THE
BEST THINGS
IN LIFE

> ## A CONTEMPORARY SOCRATES LOOKS AT POWER, PLEASURE, TRUTH & THE GOOD LIFE

PETER
KREEFT

IVP Books

An imprint of InterVarsity Press
Downers Grove, Illinois

InterVarsity Press
P.O. Box 1400, Downers Grove, IL 60515-1426
World Wide Web: www.ivpress.com
E-mail: mail@ivpress.com

InterVarsity Press® *is the book-publishing division of InterVarsity Christian Fellowship/USA*®*, a student movement active on campus at hundreds of universities, colleges and schools of nursing in the United States of America, and a member movement of the International Fellowship of Evangelical Students. For information about local and regional activities, write Public Relations Dept., InterVarsity Christian Fellowship/USA, 6400 Schroeder Rd., P.O. Box 7895, Madison, WI 53707-7895, or visit the IVCF website at* <*www.intervarsity.org*>.

Cover illustration: Joe DeVelasco

ISBN-10: 0-87784-922-6
ISBN-13: 978-0-87784-922-3

Printed in the United States of America ∞

Library of Congress Cataloging-in-Publication Data

Kreeft, Peter.
    The best things in life.

    1. College students—Conduct of life—Miscellanea.
I. Title.
BJ1661.K68   1984   170'.44   84-6697
ISBN 0-87784-922-6

P	35	34	33	32	31	30	29	28	27	26	25
Y	20	19	18	17	16	15	14	13	12	11	10

For Jim Sire,
Socrates to my Socrates

CONTENTS

Preface

What is the old Greek philosopher Socrates doing on the campus of Desperate State University? you may ask. And how did he get there? And is this the real Socrates or only an imitation?

The answer to the first question is clear: Socrates is doing at Desperate State just what he did in Athens: being Socratic. Even death did not change Socrates; his philosophizing was indeed, as he hoped, "a rehearsal for dying." How many of us have such job security even after death? In his *Apology* Socrates expressed his hope that he would be allowed to go on cross-examining people even after death. Here he gets his wish.

As to the second question, how he got here, I have no idea. I awoke one morning with my head full of Socrates and I cannot shake him loose from any place I go, especially my place of work. You see, I am a college philosophy teacher. Socrates would probably call me an intellectual prostitute, a Sophist, since I get paid for it. Imagine selling wisdom for a fee!

Finally, as to the third question, is this the real Socrates or only an imitation? Only you, the reader, can judge that.

However he got here, here he is, the wonderful troublemaker, the gadfly of Athens who makes difficulties everywhere, especially where life is too easy for thought or thought too easy for honesty. Here he is, the philosopher without a system, the question-wielding swordsman of the mind, the one infected by the oracle's puzzle, spreading his good infection, questioning, under the conviction that "the unexamined life is not worth living."

Peter Kreeft
Boston College

Foreword
by Anytus of Athens

I don't know why they let me write this foreword, because I'm going to tell you why *not* to read this book. This is a warning. If you know what's good for your society, you will throw this book into the fire and bomb the publishing plant.

I know this fellow Socrates. I have had dealings with him before. I was one of the three who tried to save our beloved Athens by getting Socrates executed. But it was too late.

This man may seem to you a harmless crank, even a wise man, perhaps; but he can tear down a whole society, I assure you. He did it to ours. He taught us to question our old gods, the foundation of our state. He will pull down yours, too, if you listen to him. This very book dethrones the two great gods of your society, Power and Pleasure, and puts in their place only a vague, invisible deity Socrates will not even name.

I remember he used to speak of this "unknown god" in Athens. We worshiped many gods, but not Socrates. We named many gods, but not Socrates. We accepted our traditions unquestioningly, but not Socrates. He even once sculpted a pedestal without a statue and cut the inscription "to the unknown god." (He was a stone-cutter.) It was the very inscription that rabble-rouser Paul of Tarsus referred to when he preached to the philosophers on Mars Hill, where the statues of the gods stood.

You may have read that story in your Scriptures—Acts 17. Paul connected his God and Socrates' god this way: he said, "the god you worship in ignorance I now declare to you." It was the same God, the destroyer of secular utopias—yours as well as ours. Paul's was the final step in tearing down our state—the Christian infection—but Socrates prepared the downfall with his first step. Socrates questioned the old gods; Paul introduced the new God. If Socrates had not dethroned the old, there would have been no searching, no room for the new. I warn you, he will do the same thing to you.

I.
SOCRATES
AND PETER PRAGMA

1 On Education and E.T.

Socrates: Excuse me for bothering you, but what are you doing?

Peter Pragma: What kind of silly question is that? I'm reading a book. Or was, until you interrupted me. Can't you see that?

Socrates: Alas, I often fail to see what others see, and see things others cannot see.

Peter: I don't get it.

Socrates: I saw you holding the book, yes, but I did not see you reading it.

Peter: What in the world are you talking about?

Socrates: You are holding the book in your hands, aren't you?

Peter: Of course.

Socrates: And I can see your hands.

Peter: So?

Socrates: But do you read the book with your hands?

Peter: Of course not.

Socrates: With what, then?

Peter: With my eyes, of course.

Socrates: Oh, I don't think so.

Peter: I think you're crazy.

Socrates: Perhaps, but I speak the truth, and I think I can show you that. Tell me, can a corpse read?

Peter: No...

Socrates: But a corpse can have eyes, can't it?

Peter: Yes.

Socrates: Then it is not just the eyes that read.

Peter: Oh. The mind then. Are you satisfied now?

Socrates: No.

Peter: Somehow I thought you'd say that.

Socrates: I cannot see your mind, can I?

Peter: No.

Socrates: Then I cannot see you reading.

Peter: I guess you can't. But what a strange thing to say!

Socrates: Strange but true. Truth is often stranger than fiction, you know. Which do you prefer?

Peter: You know, you're stranger than fiction too, little man.

Socrates: That's because I'm true too.

Peter: Who are you, anyway?

Socrates: I am Socrates.

Peter: Sure you are. And I'm E.T.

Socrates: I'm pleased to meet you, E.T.

Peter: My name is Peter Pragma.

Socrates: Do you have two names?

Peter: What do you mean?

Socrates: You said your name was E.T.

Peter: And you said your name was Socrates.

Socrates: Because it is. I have this strange habit of saying what is.

Peter: What do you want from me?

Socrates: Would you let me pursue my silly question just a moment longer?

Peter: I thought you got your answer.

Socrates: Not to my real question. You see, when I asked you what you were doing, I really meant, *Why* are you doing it?

Peter: I'm studying for my exam tomorrow.

Socrates: And why are you doing *that*?

Peter: You know, you sound like a little child.

Socrates: Thank you.

Peter: I didn't mean it as a compliment.

Socrates: I don't care. Only answer the question, please.

Peter: I'm studying to pass my course, of course.

Socrates: And why do you want to do that?

Peter: Another silly question! Don't you ever grow up?

Socrates: Let me tell you a secret, Peter: there *are* no grown-ups. But you still haven't answered my "silly question."

Peter: To get a degree, of course.

Socrates: You mean all the time and effort and money you put into your education here at Desperate State is to purchase that little piece of paper?

Peter: That's the way it is.

Socrates: I think you may be able to guess what my next question is going to be.

Peter: I'm catching on. I think it's an infection.

Socrates: What is the next question, then?

Peter: You're going to ask me why I want a degree.

Socrates: And you're going to answer.

Peter: But it's another silly question. Everyone knows what a degree is for.

Socrates: But I am not "everyone." So would you please tell me?

Peter: A college degree is the entrance ticket to a good job. Do you know how difficult the job market is today? Where have you been for the last few years?

Socrates: You wouldn't believe me if I told you. But we must ask just one more question, or rather two: What is "a good job" and why do you want one?

Peter: Money, of course. That's the answer to both questions. To all questions, maybe.

Socrates: I see. And what do you want to do with all the money you make?

Peter: You said your last two questions were your last.

Socrates: If you want to go away, I cannot keep you here. But if we pursue our explorations one little step further, we may discover something new.

Peter: What do you think you'll find? A new world?

Socrates: Quite possibly. A new world of thought. Will you come with me? Shall we trudge ahead through the swamps of our uncertainties? Or shall we sit comfortably at home in our little cave?

Peter: Why should I torture myself with all these silly questions from a strange little man? I'm supposed to be studying for my exam.

Socrates: Because it would be profitable for you. The unexamined life is not worth living, you know.

Peter: I heard that somewhere . . . Good grief! That's one of the quotations that might be on my exam tomorrow. Who said that, anyway?

Socrates: I did. Didn't you hear me?

Peter: No, I mean who said it originally?

Socrates: It was I, I assure you. Now shall we continue our journey?

Peter: What are you getting at, anyway, Socrates?

Socrates: No, Peter, the question is what *you* are getting at. That is the topic we were exploring. Now shall we continue to make your life a little less unexamined and a little more worth living?

Peter: All right. For a little while, anyway.

Socrates: Then you will answer my last question?

Peter: I forgot what it was.

Socrates: What do you need money for?

Peter: Everything! Everything I want costs money.

Socrates: For instance?

Peter: Do you know how much it costs to raise a family nowadays?

Socrates: And what would you say is the largest expense in raising a family nowadays?

Peter: Probably sending the kids to college.

Socrates: I see. Let's review what you have said. You are reading this book to study for your exam, so that you can pass it and your course, to graduate and get a degree, to get a good job, to make a lot of money, to raise a family and send your children to college.

Peter: Right.

Socrates: And why will they go to college?

Peter: Same reason I'm here. To get good jobs, of course.

Socrates: So they can send their children to college?

Peter: Yes.

Socrates: Have you ever heard the expression "arguing in a circle"?

Peter: No, I never took logic.

Socrates: Really? I would never have guessed it.

Peter: You're teasing me.

Socrates: Really?

Peter: I'm a practical man. I don't care about logic, just life.

Socrates: Then perhaps we should call what you are doing "living in a circle." Have you ever asked yourself a terrifying, threatening question? What is the whole circle there for?

Peter: Hmmm . . . nobody ever bothered me with that question before.

Socrates: I know. That is why I was sent to you.

Peter: Well, sending kids to college isn't the only thing I'm working for. I'm working for my own good too. That's not circle, is it?

Socrates: We don't know until we look, do we? Tell me, wh

is "your own good"?

Peter: What do you mean?

Socrates: What benefit to yourself do you hope the money from a well-paying job will bring you?

Peter: All sorts of things. The good life. Fun and games. Leisure.

Socrates: I see. And you are now giving up fun and games for some serious studying so that you can pass your exams and your courses and get your degree.

Peter: Right. It's called "delayed gratification." I could be watching the football game right now, or playing poker. But I'm putting my time in the bank. It's an investment for the future. You see, when I'm set up in a good job, I'll be able to call my own shots.

Socrates: You mean you will then have leisure and be able to watch football games or play poker whenever you wish.

Peter: Right.

Socrates: Why don't you just do those things right now?

Peter: What?

Socrates: Why do you work instead of play if all you want to do is play? You're working now so that years from now you can have enough money to afford leisure to play. But you can play now. So why take the long, hard road if you're already home? It seems to be another circle back to where you started from, where you are now.

Peter: Are you telling me I should just drop out of school and goof off?

Socrates: No, I am telling you that you should find a good reason to be here. I don't think you have found that yet. Shall we keep searching?

Peter: All right, wise man, or wise guy, whichever you are. You tell me. Why should I be here? What's the value of college? You've got a sermon up your sleeve, haven't you?

Socrates: Is that what you expect me to do?

Peter: Sure. Didn't you just tear down my answers so that you

could sell me yours?

Socrates: Indeed not. I am not a wise man, only a philosopher, a lover and pursuer of wisdom, that divine but elusive goal.

Peter: What do you want with me then?

Socrates: To spread the infection of philosophizing.

Peter: So you're not going to teach me the answers?

Socrates: No. I think the most valuable lesson I could teach you is to become your own teacher. Isn't that one of the things you are here to learn? Isn't that one of the greatest values of a college education? Have none of your teachers taught you that? What has become of my great invention, anyway?

Peter: I guess I never looked at education that way.

Socrates: It's not too late to begin.

Peter: It is today, Socrates—or whoever you are. I'm really too busy today.

Socrates: Too busy to know why you're so busy? Too busy doing to know what you're doing?

Peter: Look, maybe we could continue this conversation some other time. I have more important things to do than this stuff . . .

Socrates: Philosophy. This stuff is philosophy. What exam are you studying for, by the way?

Peter: Well, actually, it's a philosophy exam.

Socrates: I see. I think you may be in trouble there.

Peter: No way. I memorized the professor's notes. I've got all the answers.

Socrates: And none of the questions. What is the value of your answers then?

Peter: I just can't waste time on questions like that.

Socrates: Because you have to study philosophy?

Peter: Yes. Good-by, strange little man.

Socrates: Good-by, E.T. I hope some day you escape your circular wanderings and find your way home.

2 On Liberal Education and Careers

Socrates: Hello, Peter.

Peter: You again! I thought I had escaped you.

Socrates: You were mistaken! You cannot escape yourself.

Peter: You mean you are a part of me, somehow?

Socrates: Yes, somehow. How did you do on your exam yesterday?

Peter: Terrible! I kept getting confused—by my memory of you.

Socrates: That often happens; philosophizing can play havoc with philosophy. What are you doing now with all those papers and catalogs?

Peter: Planning next semester's courses. It's registration time.

Socrates: You look perplexed.

Peter: I've got to do some serious thinking before I choose my major.

Socrates: Perhaps I can help. Thinking's my thing, you might say.

Peter: Perhaps you can. You see, I'm at a turning point in my education, and maybe in my life. I can't decide between Business and Science as my major. But how could you help me to make that choice? It's not *your* choice.

Socrates: No, but I might help you apply the world's most practical tool for making choices.

Peter: Sounds good. What's that?

Socrates: Logic.

Peter: Already it's sounding worse. How is logic practical? How would it help me choose?

Socrates: It would tell us first to examine the nature of choice in general, then apply the principles of choosing to your particular choice. Shall we look?

Peter: I guess I need all the help I can get. So I'll endure your silly questions again, even though they left me with all questions and no answers last time. Maybe this time we'll make some progress.

Socrates: Oh, but we made enormous progress last time. Lesson One is usually much harder to learn than Lesson Two.

Peter: What do you mean?

Socrates: I think you know.

Peter: You mean Lesson One is questions and Lesson Two is answers?

Socrates: Yes. See what a quick learner you are? A quick starter, at least. It took me a lifetime to fully realize Lesson One.

Peter: So let's get started on Lesson Two.

Socrates: Hmmm. Perhaps you are not such a quick learner after all. Do you really think you have already learned in one day what took me a lifetime?

Peter: Well, no, I don't have all your answers yet...

Socrates: You don't have my *questions* yet.

Peter: Oh, all right. Let's look at the questions first.

Socrates: A reasonable thing for one in search of answers, don't you think? They are the road, and only those who use the road find their way home. Well, then, let us ask about choosing. Would you agree that whenever we have to choose between two good things—whether really or apparently good—both must seem attractive?

Peter: Yes.

Socrates: So we should look at the different ways things are attractive.

Peter: But aren't there thousands?

Socrates: I think they can be reduced to two. A thing may be or seem good for something else, like a tool, or good for itself: a means or an end. Do you agree?

Peter: No. What's good for itself?

Socrates: What about happiness? Do we choose happiness as a means to anything else—riches, or pleasure, or reputation? Don't we choose all those things as means to happiness?

Peter: I guess we do. But how does that help me choose between business and science?

Socrates: How impatient you are! Do you seek these two things as means or ends?

Peter: Means, I guess.

Socrates: Then we must consider two questions: what ends they serve and how well they serve those ends. If one of them helps you to a better end, or better helps you to the same end, it would be the better thing to choose, wouldn't it?

Peter: Oh. Yes indeed. How obvious. Why didn't I think of that?

Socrates: Perhaps because you were so busy looking at science and business that you neglected philosophy.

Peter: Philosophy! That's not my thing. That liberal arts stuff is for the snobs.

Socrates: Snobs?

Peter: Sure. Rich people with leisure. I've got no time for that.

I have to plan to get a good job when I graduate. What good can philosophy help me to do?

Socrates: Define "good."

Peter: You mean... philosophy can help me define "good"?

Socrates: Exactly. And unless you know what "good" is you can't tell what "a good job" is, can you? And if you can't tell what a good job is, how do you expect to find one?

Peter: I know what a good job is. It's one that makes a lot of money.

Socrates: One that would enable you to become rich and leisured?

Peter: Right.

Socrates: Would you then be a snob?

Peter: No.

Socrates: Then you were wrong to define a snob as someone with riches and leisure.

Peter: Look here, are you out to help me or to insult me?

Socrates: Are you sure those two things are "either/or"?

Peter: Socrates, I can't take any more of this cleverness. I'm a practical person, and I'm concerned with practical things like making money. Now if you really want to help me, just accept me as I am and let's talk about careers.

Socrates: All right, let's talk about practical things. Take money, for instance....

Peter: Gladly. Now you're talking.

Socrates: If you couldn't buy anything with it—if all your money were counterfeit or out of date—then it would be good for nothing, wouldn't it?

Peter: Of course.

Socrates: So money is good only as a means, not as an end.

Peter: It's good for whatever money can buy. And that's a pretty big piece of the pie.

Socrates: So you are interested in these courses, in science or business, as means to getting a good job, and the job as a means to making money, and the money as a means to buying "a piece of the pie," right?

Peter: Right on target.

Socrates: So you see what question logic leads us to ask next?

Peter: The pie?

Socrates: Now you are on target too. Yes. Those things you hope to buy with your money—is any one of them an end in itself? A car, for instance? Or a house?

Peter: I don't know. I never thought of that.

Socrates: That is precisely what I am here to remedy. Isn't a car called a *"means* of transportation"?

Peter: Yes.

Socrates: And isn't a house a means to shelter you and your family and your possessions?

Peter: Yes.

Socrates: Then we must ask: transportation for what end? Shelter for what end?

Peter: Oh, I don't know. It's too complicated. One thing I do know, though. Liberal arts aren't going to help me get what I want.

Socrates: How do you know that if you don't know what you want? And might not liberal arts help you to know what you want?

Peter: I don't know.

Socrates: Good. You are learning Lesson One. Shall we proceed to Lesson Two and try to find out what you do want?

Peter: Please!

Socrates: Well, then, to begin with, do you think it is in any way the same as what everyone wants? Do you think there is any common or universal end sought by everyone? Or do you think each one seeks a totally different end?

Peter: Different strokes for different folks, they say.

Socrates: Do you see nothing common to all these "different strokes"?

Peter: No. Do you?

Socrates: Don't we all seek happiness, and pleasure, and joy?

Peter: Oh, of course. But that's abstract. Nothing concrete is universal.

Socrates: What about food and drink and health and the preservation of life?

Peter: Oh, of course. Our *bodies* all need the same things. But that's all.

Socrates: What about love and friendship and companionship and escape from loneliness?

Peter: All right, so we share some common ends. So what? How does that help me choose between business and science?

Socrates: Are you concerned mainly with what will benefit yourself?

Peter: Yes. I look out for Number One. Anything wrong with that?

Socrates: I did not say there was. But from the sharp tone of your answer, I suspect you think there is. Perhaps we could investigate that question some other day. But for now, I think I can show you that a liberal education can bring you great benefit—perhaps even more than science or business.

Peter: No way.

Socrates: You know that for certain, do you?

Peter: Yep.

Socrates: Perhaps Lesson One has not been learned after all. Shall we look at this thing that you know for certain, just to be sure we do not miss something?

Peter: I've looked already. Forget it.

Socrates: But even when we look, do we not sometimes overlook? Isn't it worth taking a few more minutes to look one more time, just to be sure you didn't miss something that might be of great benefit to you?

Peter: Oh, all right. What do you want to look at?

Socrates: At the benefits science and business can bring you, and then at the benefits of the liberal arts, and then at a comparison between them.

Peter: We already looked at business. It would teach me to make a mint.

Socrates: And that road led to a dead end, remember? Unless you have an answer now to the question about means and ends —a live end, so to speak.

Peter: No. Let's look at science.

Socrates: All right. What attracts you there?

Peter: Same thing. Money. Science is where the big bucks are. The dough.

Socrates: Hmmm. And the bucks mate with the doe and make more bucks and doe? A deer park.

Peter: It's dear, all right. It's hire education.

Socrates: I see you're catching my appundicitis as well as my good infection of philosophizing. Well, then, it seems pretty straightforward: if your only end is money and you won't consider any further end, then whatever means is more likely to attain this monetary end is what you want. It is a mere calculation of probabilities. Are you sure that's all you care about?

Peter: Well . . . I'd kinda like to do something worthwhile while I'm worth millions. You know, helping humanity and all that. I don't see why I can't do well and do good at the same time, do you?

Socrates: No indeed. But that factor complicates your calculation a bit. It means you must ask a second question about science and business: which helps humanity more?

Peter: That's why I'm hesitating. Business will make me rich faster, I think, but science seems better in the other way. A sort of higher calling. I thought of medicine or psychology or social work, too, but they don't turn me on like science.

Socrates: And what is the value to humanity you see in science? Is it the search for truth?

Peter: Come on, now. What century are you from?

Socrates: You would not believe me if I told you. But what does the century have to do with the truth? Do you tell truth with a calendar?

Peter: Socrates, in the twentieth century the point of science is not some abstract "truth" but power, control of the forces of nature. Our time doesn't think about "truth" anymore.

Socrates: I wonder how time can think. I thought only people did that.

Peter: The people of our century, then.

Socrates: All of them?

Peter: Almost.

Socrates: What about the scientists? Do they think science is for power rather than truth?

Peter: I don't know. Some do and some don't. I don't care about that. *I* think so. That would be my motive for going into Science, and we're supposed to be helping me decide, aren't we?

Socrates: Yes.

Peter: Well, that's what I'd go into: practical science, not theoretical science. Technology.

Socrates: All right. So far we have mentioned three areas of study for you: business, practical science, or technology, and liberal arts. Do you see what each can give you?

Peter: Sure. Business gives me money, technology gives me power, and liberal arts give me a pain,

Socrates: Let us look at power for a minute. I wonder whether it will be a dead end, too, like money. Power is a means, isn't it?

Peter: Yes.

Socrates: Then what is the end to which the powers of technology are means?

Peter: Making the world a better place to live in. Cars and rockets and bridges and artificial organs and Pac-Man.

Socrates: So technology improves material things in the world.

Peter: Yes. Including our own bodies. Pretty important, don't you think?

Socrates: Oh, yes. But I wonder whether there might not be something even more important to us. If we could improve our own lives, our own actions, our own behavior—wouldn't this concern us even more intimately than improving the world outside us?

Peter: Why?

Socrates: Because its benefit would be closer to home, so to speak.

Peter: I see. Yes. I guess that's why I'm attracted to business. Making my life a little better is more practical to me than making bridges or rockets. So business is better than technology, right?

Socrates: Well, not necessarily "better" in an absolute and unqualified way, especially if we use "good" and "better" without defining them. But from your point of view, business seems to improve something closer to you than technology does: an aspect of your own life. Politics and ethics would do the same, in a much more fundamental way.

Peter: Politics and ethics? No way. I want something practical.

Socrates: Oh, politics and ethics are quite practical. They teach us how to practice, how to act. Aristotle called them "practical sciences" and technology "productive science." Practical sciences improve our practice; productive sciences improve our products. Economics is a practical science.

Peter: Then I guess it's economics and business for me.

Socrates: For that reason? That it improves something closer to yourself?

Peter: Yes. I look out for Number One.

Socrates: Then you should choose Liberal Arts, for the same reason.

Peter: What?

Socrates: I said . . .

Peter: I heard what you said. I just couldn't believe it. It's silly.

Socrates: "Silly" may be in the eye of the beholder. Look here, if you could find some study that improved something even closer to yourself than the practical sciences, you should prefer that, shouldn't you?

Peter: Yes, but you said liberal arts. That's way out in left field.

Socrates: Let's see. What is the purpose of the liberal arts?

Peter: Who knows?

Socrates: You, I hope. If not, let's remedy that.

Peter: I guess they're for culture. A veneer of upper-class respectability. For snobs, not slobs.

Socrates: You are so wrong that for once I will simply tell you the right answer. The liberal arts seek knowledge for its own sake.

Peter: That's even farther out. Out of my ballpark. That "knowledge for its own sake" stuff may be a turn-on for you philosophers, but not for me.

Socrates: Are you quite sure? Look at your own standard again. How did you rank the sciences?

Peter: By how close to home they came. And liberal arts is out by the left-field foul pole.

Socrates: Let's see. Productive sciences improve what?

Peter: Things in the world.

Socrates: And practical sciences improve what?

Peter: My practice.

Socrates: And knowledge for the sake of knowledge improves what?

Peter: Nothing.

Socrates: Don't you see that it improves something closer to you than your practice?

Peter: No. What?

Socrates: What is the closest thing to yourself?

Peter: My underwear, I guess.

Socrates: Your self, is it not? Your *you*, your identity, your personality, your psyche, your soul, your consciousness, your mind. Do you have any idea what I'm referring to? You look puzzled.

Peter: I think you're talking about something more than my good looks, but I have trouble seeing that far inside. I guess you mean the liberal arts are supposed to give me some sort of "expansion of consciousness," right?

Socrates: You could call it that, yes. I called it a liberation from the cave of ignorance. Almost like birth, or waking up: popping your mind out of its womblike dreams into the light of reality.

Peter: My liberal arts courses never gave me that.

Socrates: Then the fault was either with the teacher or with the student, but not with the subject.

Peter: But what could I do with liberal arts?

Socrates: The question is rather what they could do with you?

Peter: No, I want business or science. Forget it.

Socrates: You can take both.

Peter: I'm forced to. The college has those silly required courses.

Socrates: For a good reason, as we have just seen. And here is a second one: whatever career you choose—science or business or anything else—you also have a second career as well, and liberal arts help you in that.

Peter: You mean I'll have to moonlight?

Socrates: No, I mean you can't just be a businessman or a scientist or a technician. You must also be something else. Do you see what?

Peter: No.

Socrates: All the more need then. A human being, is what. That is our common career. And the liberal arts help you to *that* end.

Peter: How?

Socrates: They investigate the question I devoted my whole life to: "know thyself." Was it not your concern with yourself that you were using as your standard in choosing what courses were most important?

Peter: Well, yes, but...

Socrates: But?

Peter: "Know thyself" is fine for philosophers, but we slobs need diversions.

Socrates: Don't we also need truth?

Peter: Pac-Man's more fun, you know.

Socrates: It isn't, you know. I've tried both. Have you?

Peter: You question everything, don't you?

Socrates: Yes, especially the most important thing. Long ago I said "the unexamined life is not worth living." You seem to be saying now that the examined life is not worth living. Is that what you think?

Peter: I don't know what I think.

Socrates: Well, that's Lesson One, anyway.

Peter: I guess I haven't gotten far into Lesson Two yet. Somehow I know I'm not finished with you, Socrates.

Socrates: Or with yourself, I hope.

Peter: Let me go get a cup of coffee to clear my head of all these cobwebs...

Socrates: You mean these logical thoughts.

Peter: I'll be back in a little while, O.K.?

Socrates: I won't be far away.

3 On Technology and Inchworms

Peter: Socrates, I'm back.

Socrates: Without your coffee, I see.

Peter: The darn machine was broken. And I want to know how to fix it. I'm going to be a technician.

Socrates: You've decided, then.

Peter: Yes.

Socrates: Why have you come to me, then? You know I like to upset your little applecarts with my bothersome questions. Might it be that you're not quite certain yet? One broken coffee machine isn't quite an adequate reason for choosing a career, is it?

Peter: You're right. But I can't stand any more quizzing today. Is there any other way you can help me look at technology without quizzing me?

Socrates: Hmmm... perhaps there is a way.

Peter: You mean you're actually going to give me answers instead of questions, finally? I don't believe it!

Socrates: Oh, no. I know of no way to answers except through questions.

Peter: I thought it sounded too good to be true.

Socrates: But you might listen as I ask someone else, someone already in the career you want to explore. How about that?

Peter: A great idea. Let's visit the science labs. They're right over here. The university is doing some research for the government—on genetics, I think. Here—look at all these people at work. Maybe you can find one to be your guinea pig.

Socrates: How about the lady over there by the window?

Peter: You mean the one working with the guinea pigs?

Socrates: Yes. . . . Pardon me, Miss. Do you have a moment to talk with us?

Marigold Measurer: Sure thing. My name is Marigold. Who are you and what do you want to know?

Socrates: I'm Socrates, and this is my friend Peter Pragma, and we'd like to know what you're doing here.

Marigold: My daily work, of course. What are *you* doing here asking such a silly question?

Socrates: *My* daily work.

Marigold: I don't understand.

Peter: I'm thinking of a career in technology, and I thought I could sort of interview you, if you don't mind. But my friend Socrates asks questions better than I do, so I'd rather listen and let him talk.

Marigold: I'll be glad to help you if I can, Peter. But what are you, Socrates, some kind of head shrinker?

Socrates: Some kind of head expander, you might say. I am a philosopher.

Marigold: Oh, one of those. Why aren't you over in the philosophy department, then, where you belong?

Socrates: Because there is no "philosophy department."

Marigold: Sure there is. It's the second building on your left. You can't miss it.

Socrates: No, I mean that a "philosophy department" is a contradiction in terms. Philosophy is not a department.

Marigold: I don't get it. Of course it is.

Socrates: Do you think of life as a kind of department store, where the customer wanders in and randomly chooses to shop in some departments and not others?

Marigold: Sort of. What's wrong with that? It's a free country.

Socrates: But not a free universe. I mean that some questions are unavoidable because they deal not with some optional department of life. They are the philosophical questions.

Marigold: Hmph! You think your work is superior to mine?

Socrates: I don't know. That depends on what yours is.

Marigold: No it doesn't. It depends on whether you're antediluvian enough to be an elitist.

Socrates: Do you mean to say that every work is really just as important as every other?

Marigold: Sure. It's a democracy, you know.

Socrates: A democracy of works as well as people?

Marigold: Why not?

Socrates: Aren't some works necessarily subordinate to others, as means to ends? For instance, I was once a stonecutter, and my work served a greater work, that of the architect, which in turn served the greater work of city planning and ruling, or politics. How can the end not be more important than the means?

Marigold: Are you saying the end justifies the means?

Socrates: No, I am saying just what I am saying, neither more nor less. That's a rather difficult art, you know. And another difficult and rare art is to hear it.

Marigold: What did you say, then?

Socrates: I said, How can the end not be more important than the means? At least, that's what I thought I said. Is my memory failing me after only 2453 years?

Marigold: I don't know what you're talking about. I just know I don't buy that old idea of hierarchy among people.

Socrates: What about hierarchy among works?

Marigold: Works are done by people. So if you say a stone-cutter's work is subordinate to an architect's, you end up saying the stonecutter is subordinate to the architect.

Socrates: Do you think that logically follows?

Marigold: I just don't believe people are inferior just because they're subordinates.

Socrates: Oh, neither do I. Perhaps we really agree, if only we keep in mind two distinctions: first, between people and their works, and second, between subordination and inferiority. Then we can admit some works are subordinate to others without implying that the people who perform them are inferior.

Marigold: O.K., I guess.

Socrates: Now can we return to Peter's question? What work are you doing here?

Marigold: Not philosophy, that's for sure.

Socrates: We shall see about that.

Marigold: My work is something you can do something with. Genetic engineering. I'm fitting these guinea pigs with blue genes. It's part of the great work of the conquest of nature by science. What can you do with philosophy, anyway?

Socrates: We can use it to examine your work.

Marigold: But it bakes no bread.

Socrates: I certainly hope not. What a strange philosopher it would be who used an oven instead of a mind!

Marigold: Your work may conquer thoughts, but mine conquers nature.

Socrates: Why do you want to *conquer* nature? Why not befriend her instead?

Marigold: Her?

Socrates: Do not the poets tell us nature is our mother? Why would you want to conquer your mother? We conquer our enemies.

Marigold: Nature is not my mother, nor is it my enemy. It is simply matter, raw material to be improved.

Socrates: To what end?

Marigold: Human happiness. My work makes a happier world. Do you deny that fire, the wheel, the domestication of animals, anesthetics and antibiotics constitute progress?

Socrates: No. But perhaps my work can effect an even greater progress.

Marigold: How? What can it conquer?

Socrates: The conqueror. You conquer nature, but do you control your own control?

Marigold: You mean I should be afraid of losing control of nature?

Socrates: No, of yourself. Isn't that why the people of this century are fascinated with the image of Frankenstein's monster? Don't you feel as if you are the Sorcerer's apprentice who just recently discovered the Master's book of magic spells but who is not yet wise and mature enough to use them well? Isn't your work like giving society a much faster and more powerful vehicle just at the time when it has thrown away all the road maps?

Marigold: I didn't do anything to the road maps. I just make the vehicles. All this stuff about Frankenstein's monster and the Sorcerer's apprentice is irrelevant. My work is nothing like magic. It's sober science.

Socrates: You may be sober, but what of those who use the powers you discover? The winemaker may be sober but should he supply to drunks?

Marigold: You mean our society is drunk with power? Why do you think that?

Socrates: Do you not receive a substantial salary for your work?

Marigold: Of course.

Peter: Just how much do you make, if you don't mind my asking?

Marigold: A lot more than philosophers do. I work for the government, and it doesn't employ many philosophers.

Socrates: What a pity. And your government is representative of your society, isn't it?

Marigold: Yes.

Socrates: So your large salary reflects your society's values, then?

Marigold: Yes. It values my work quite highly.

Socrates: Why? Is it not because of the powers you hope to give it?

Marigold: Yes...

Socrates: So you might call your society one drunk with the lust for power. But it's hard to argue about such a vague and nebulous thing as "society." Perhaps we should investigate the other term you used to describe your work. "Sober *science,*" you call it. But is your work science or technology?

Marigold: How do you distinguish the two?

Socrates: The aim of science is simply to know. *Science*—from *scio,* "I know." The aim of technology is the conquest of nature. *Technology*—from *technē,* "know-how." A kind of sober magic, you might say.

Marigold: I might not. Magic is an ancient superstition. Both science and technology are modern and enlightened. They have nothing to do with magic.

Socrates: So you think the spirit of technology is closer to the spirit of science than to the spirit of magic?

Marigold: Of course. Everyone knows that.

Socrates: I suppose I am no one, then, for I do not know that. In fact, I seem to know just the opposite.

Marigold: What? That's ridiculous.

Socrates: Well, let me tell you why I have this ridiculous idea, and perhaps you can free me from its thrall. Tell me, when in your history was the great age of magic?

Marigold: The Middle Ages, of course.

Socrates. Not so. It was the Renaissance, the dawn of the modern era.

Marigold: I didn't know that.

Socrates: That's because history is one of the liberal arts, and your education has neglected them. As a matter of historical fact, interest in magic and interest in technology arose together. Magic died off simply because it didn't work very reliably, while technology did. But the same spirit motivates both: the demand to conquer nature, the lust for power.

Marigold: Well, what's wrong with that, anyway? It's better than passively sitting in your cave and praying to the gods to stop the thunder. The ancients feared nature and even worshiped it. We conquer it.

Socrates: Are there no alternatives to those two extremes? Must you either conquer something or else fear and worship it?

Marigold: What's your alternative? What do you philosophers do with nature?

Socrates: We try to understand it and befriend it. For instance, where you speak of "the conquest of space" I should prefer to speak of "the befriending of space." Though I should also prefer to speak of "the heavens" rather than "space." . . .

Marigold: You're ridiculously out of date, you know.

Socrates: Thank you.

Marigold: I didn't mean it as a compliment. Why do you feel so superior?

Socrates: I think we premodern philosophers had a better relation with nature because we had a better answer to an even greater question, the question of the *summum bonum*, the greatest good, the most important thing in life.

Peter: Now there's a question for you! Some day you shall have to help me explore that question, Socrates.

Socrates: Why, Peter, you're becoming a philosopher.

Marigold: Hey, wait, you two. What was your old answer to the question of the *summum bonum*? What's more important than the conquest of nature? And weren't there thousands of different answers, different religions and philosophies and myths and creeds and codes and cults?

Socrates: Yes, but they all had one motive in common, which is the opposite of your technology.

Marigold: A single motive? Why isn't it obvious then? I don't see it.

Socrates: Perhaps because it's too obvious for inchworm eyes to notice.

Marigold: Enough! What is it?

Socrates: They all agreed that the most important thing in life was somehow to conform the human soul to objective reality. Your "conquest of nature" philosophy thinks the most important thing is to conform objective reality to the desires of the human soul.

Marigold: But that's progress. It sure beats worshiping stones and stars.

Socrates: Oh, but the ancients didn't worship nature. That would be ridiculously unnatural. They worshiped gods, or God. The "objective reality" they tried to conform their soul to was not stones or even stars but gods, or God, or the will of God, or the laws of God. Even when the philosophers substituted Justice for Zeus and Beauty for Aphrodite and Truth for Apollo, the great task of human life remained essentially the same: to conform the soul to these divine, superhuman realities. They thought objective reality was much more than the material world, you see. So their life view quite logically followed their world view. Do you understand that?

Marigold: No.

Socrates: Well, if you believe there *is* something superior to man, it makes sense to try to become like it, doesn't it?

Marigold: It was passivity. Conformity.

Socrates: Would it make sense to try to conquer a god?

Marigold: No, but suppose there are no gods? If the only thing outside us is nature, and nature is unconscious matter, then you try to get it to conform to you, not vice versa.

Socrates: My point exactly. Do you see the principle common to both beliefs?

Marigold: No. What do you mean?

Socrates: That the lower should conform to the higher. The principle of hierarchy that you denied a moment ago.

Marigold: How did I deny it? I forgot what I said.

Socrates: You said that my work, philosophizing, couldn't possibly be superior to your work, technology, because there is no hierarchy of superior and inferior.

Marigold: I still say that. And even if there is superiority, it is my work that is superior. At least I have a reliable method. I *make* nature conform to my wishes by my technology. How do you make yourself conform to this vague superhuman something of yours by your philosophy?

Socrates: In a way superior to yours, a way you cannot use to make nature conform to you.

Marigold: How's that?

Socrates: Freely.

Marigold: What do you mean?

Socrates: Nature can be forced to conform to our will because it has no will of its own, isn't that right?

Marigold: Right.

Socrates: But we cannot be forced to conform to God if we have a free will.

Marigold: Right. That's why your method is so unreliable. You only preach. I practice.

Peter: She's got you there, Socrates.

Socrates: You heard your magic word, Peter. But might it not be that the very "unreliability" of my method that you scorn is proof if its superiority?

Marigold: Ridiculous. How could that be?

Socrates: Tell me, would you say a person is superior to a stone?

Marigold: In some ways, of course.

Socrates: In what ways?

Marigold: All the things a person can do that a stone can't.

Socrates: Including freedom of choice?

Marigold: Yes.

Socrates: So freedom is superior to nonfreedom?

Marigold: Yes.

Socrates: Then philosophy's method is superior to technology's. For the method of philosophy is the free appeal to a free mind, while the method of technology is to coerce an unfree nature.

Marigold: Hmmm. I never thought of that.

Socrates: And that shows another way philosophy is superior. We have illumined the role of technology by philosophy today, but we have not illumined the role of philosophy by technology.

Peter: By golly, Socrates. You're beginning to make some sense. I can't believe it!

Marigold: Philosophy still bakes no bread. It lacks the fire.

Socrates: But technology lacks the light.

Marigold: My profession is an honest and a useful one.

Socrates: Certainly. So is baking bread, which is a kind of technology. But it isn't the highest good, unless there are no gods.

Peter: That's the first question, isn't it, Socrates? If there are no gods, then technology is the highest thing because there's nothing to conform to, and we may as well make nature conform to us. What else is there to do?

Socrates: You are indeed becoming a philosopher, Peter. Do you want to face that first question now?

Marigold: Listen, you two, I have no time to get involved in some conversation about gods.

Socrates: That is indeed unfortunate.

Marigold: It's been nice talking to you, but . . .

Socrates: What do you mean by "nice"?

Marigold: I have to get back to my guinea pigs.

Socrates: I see: your master calls. Well, when your master frees you perhaps we can talk again. From all your bold talk, I had thought you were the master.

Peter: I think she's angry with you, Socrates. She didn't even say good-by.

Socrates: Neither did you, but for a different reason: you are still here. Does that mean you are not satisfied, as she is, simply to work on guinea pigs without questioning the value of the work?

Peter: Yes. I feel drawn to you, Socrates, even though you're a troublesome bother.

Socrates: That is because you are becoming more of a philosopher every day.

Peter: Hmmm. I don't know whether I should feel fearful or pleased.

Socrates: That is one of the many questions philosophy can help you explore. I shall return.

4 On Artificial Intelligence and College Presidents

Peter: Oh, Socrates, there you are! I need you to help me solve a problem. I decided to take another philosophy course. I guess your argument for liberal arts the other day took hold of me after all. Anyway, the first day of class the professor raised a question nobody in the class could answer, and it really bugs me.

Socrates: What is the problem and why does it bug you, Peter?

Peter: The problem is: what's the difference between human intelligence and computer intelligence—so-called natural and artificial intelligence? The problem bugs me because I think I might go into computers.

Socrates: You might turn yourself into a program, you mean? That's the only thing that goes into computers. The only language they understand.

Peter: I mean I think I've made my career choice. You've gotten me hooked on this new thing, thinking; and I've always been interested in technology; so I thought I could combine the two by going into computers. It's certainly the field of the future economically speaking—I can make my mint—and it's technology too. It's even a bit like philosophy, isn't it? Or is it? That's my question: what is artificial intelligence, anyway? Do computers think?

Socrates: Your teacher put the question in your laps but not the answer, eh?

Peter: Yes, he must be one of your disciples. A good, hard question, don't you think?

Socrates: Good, yes; hard, no.

Peter: You mean you think it's an easy one to answer?

Socrates: Yes.

Peter: Well? Don't hold me in suspense. And don't give me some unscientific answer about the soul, either. I want an answer I can verify empirically. What can human thinking do that computer thinking can't? Do you think that's an easy question to answer?

Socrates: Yes.

Peter: Well, my teacher doesn't think so. And according to him neither do thousands of other advanced thinkers today. How can that be, if the question is really so easy?

Socrates: Perhaps because they're so advanced that they have left behind and overlooked the most obvious thing of all.

Peter: What? What? Out with it!

Socrates: Artificial intelligence can't do what your natural intelligence just did.

Peter: What's that?

Socrates: What it's still doing. Don't you even know what you're doing? Stop and think for a minute.

Peter: Oh . . . oh. Asking questions, you mean?

Socrates: Congratulations. You found the hidden treasure.

Peter: But computers can ask questions if you program them to. You can design and program artificial intelligence to do anything natural intelligence can do.

Socrates: But can it question its programming?

Peter: If you program it to, yes.

Socrates: But it will never question its last programming.

Peter: No.

Socrates: But we do.

Peter: Oh. But that seems such a simple answer, Socrates. There must be something wrong with it.

Socrates: Ask a simple question; get a simple answer.

Peter: I can't refute it. But there seems to be so much evidence —not that *we're* only computers, but that the brain is exactly like a computer.

Socrates: It is. But as you just pointed out, we are not just our brains. In fact, brains are like computers in that they are instruments needing to be programmed by a person. The programmer departs at death, leaving his brain and the body it directed.

Peter: Couldn't any computer—whether our brain or any other —be programmed by another computer rather than by a person?

Socrates: Yes.

Peter: Then why do we have to speak of "persons" at all? Why not just computers?

Socrates: Because for such a chain of programming, we need a first, unprogrammed programmer, or a programmer that can question its programming and initiate new programs. Someone must push the first domino.

Peter: Sounds like a new argument for the existence of God.

Socrates: The same principle works here as there, anyway: the principle of causality: that you can't give what you don't have, that effects can't exist without adequate causes, that there can't be less in the total cause than in the effect. This principle seems to require a first cause both for nature and for intelligence, natural or artificial.

Peter: I don't know about God. Let's talk about something we know: ourselves.

Socrates: Something *you* know, perhaps. As for me, I find the self a mystery just as I find God a mystery.

Peter: I thought "know thyself" was your thing.

Socrates: It is. And why do you think I'm still at it after so many years?

Peter: Why is it so hard to know yourself, Socrates?

Socrates: Because the self is the knower. How can the subject become its own object? How can the *I* become an *it*? That's why I find God a mystery, too. The human *I* is the image of the divine *I*.

Peter: But cybernetics has done it, Socrates. Now we know how we think. The mysteries are opening up to the light of science.

Socrates: Really? Then please tell me, and end my lifelong quest: what is the *I*?

Peter: Didn't you say the self was the soul? That's what I learned about you in my philosophy course.

Socrates: Yes.

Peter: And the soul was the mind?

Socrates: Not *only* the mind, but the mind is at least the soul's eye, its light.

Peter: All right, let that qualification pass for now. And the mind is the brain. So it follows that the self is the brain. And now we know how the brain works. So we know ourselves by cybernetics.

Socrates: Whoa, there. Too fast. You slipped that last premise in under the table.

Peter: Which?

Socrates: That the mind is the brain.

Peter: What's the difference between mind and brain, then?

Socrates: The mind uses the brain, as a programmer uses a computer. My internal computer is no more me than any of my external computers are. I'm just more intimately hooked up to it.

Peter: This is getting too abstract for me. Can you make the same point more concretely?

Socrates: Hmmm. Perhaps if my simple argument cannot help you, someone else can, someone who can complexify and fudge the issue.

Peter: How could that be? How could we understand the complex more easily than the simple?

Socrates: Simplicity is often the last and hardest thing in the world to attain. Look. Here comes a man who might help us. Let's try him.

Peter: Oh, no, Socrates. That's President Factor, the head of Desperate State University.

Socrates: Excellent. What better place to look for brains than in the head? If anyone should be wise, it is likely to be your philosopher-king.

Peter: College presidents are not philosopher-kings.

Socrates: Oh? What a pity. Nevertheless I shall test his wisdom. What do you call him?

Peter: We call him "Fudge." Fudge Factor. But you should call him Mister President.

Socrates: All right. Excuse me, Mr. President . . .

Fudge Factor: Eh? What the devil are you?

Socrates: I am a philosopher. What are you?

Factor: I am the president of this university.

Socrates: So you preside over this Desperate State?

Factor: Eh? Preside? Well, sort of. Yes. What can I do for you? Are you some distinguished visitor from the East?

Socrates: In a way. Your student Peter Pragma here was having some difficulty answering his philosophy professor's question about how to distinguish human intelligence from artificial intelligence, and my answers were too simple to convince him. We thought that perhaps you would condescend to help us.

Peter: It was his idea, sir.

Factor: Well, now, I certainly would like to help you if I can, but I'm afraid cybernetics is just not my expertise.

Socrates: Do you mean you don't know the difference between human and computer intelligence?

Factor: That is not my field.

Socrates: That was not my question.

Factor: Huh? What was your question?

Socrates: Do you know how human intelligence is different from computer intelligence?

Factor: Of course.

Socrates: Well, poor Peter here doesn't. So would you do him the great service of sharing your knowledge with him?

Factor: Hmmm... you know, it's quite a coincidence that you should be talking about computers. I'm on my way to a meeting of the Board to decide whether to fully computerize the running of this university. It would save millions, especially in salaries. But there are a few diehards who are jealous of computers, and then there's the problem of the unions, who don't want us to fire anyone. But the bottom line is our finances, which are in a desperate state...

Socrates: Somehow I think I could have guessed that. Excuse me for interrupting, Mr. President, but poor Peter here is still waiting for your answer to his question.

Factor: Eh? What question?

Peter: What is the difference between human intelligence and computer intelligence?

Factor: I told you, that's not my field.

Socrates: Then you don't know?

Factor: I am not employed by this university to go around philosophizing.

Socrates: I see. You mean you are not programmed to respond in that area.

Factor: This is pointless. Good day.

Peter: Socrates, you insulted the president. See, there he goes, off in a huff.

Socrates: I'm sorry, Peter. It seems as if I further confused you instead of helping you.

Peter: How did you do that?

Socrates: Well, I was supposed to help you *distinguish* human from computer intelligence. But here, it seems, we have a fudge factor: a borderline case that makes the distinction much more difficult to see.

Peter: He does seem rather like a computer, doesn't he? Sometimes I wonder whether the whole human race is beginning to evolve into computers.

Socrates: A fascinating question. If computers are becoming more like us and we are becoming more like them...

Peter: You still didn't answer my question.

Socrates: I did, but you didn't like my answer. It was too simple. Should I try a more complex one?

Peter: Are you insulting me?

Socrates: Why do you think that?

Peter: You make it sound as if my mind, too, is like a computer: good at complexities but unable to understand something simple, like the nose on my face.

Socrates: Do you not see that you just answered your own question? You distinguished computer consciousness from human consciousness by complexity versus simplicity. You now have three answers to your question: the ability to question its most recent programming, the ability to initiate a chain of unprogrammed programming and the ability to understand the noncomplex.

Peter: I don't accept any of those answers as adequate.

Socrates: Then we have a fourth answer: the will, the ability to choose. You can even choose to be irrational.

Peter: Oh. I see.

Socrates: And there we have a fifth answer. You see, you understand. Computers merely receive, store, and supply information, like libraries. Would you say the Library of Congress understands anything?

Peter: The people in it do, and the people who wrote the books in it do.

Socrates: And that is your simplest and ultimate distinction between human and computer intelligence. It is the programmers and users of computers that understand, but not the computers.

Peter: Are you against computers, Socrates?

Socrates: Of course not. Am I against brains? But I am against confusion—against personalizing instruments and instrumentalizing persons, which is what is at stake in this philosophical question about human and computer intelligence.

Peter: I hope I see your clear and simple distinction some day, Socrates.

Socrates: So do I. For what doth it profit a man if he gain a whole data bank but lose his own self?

5 On Superstition and Santa Claus

Socrates: Are you looking for me, Peter?

Peter: As a matter of fact, I am.

Socrates: Now there's role reversal for you.

Peter: Your habit of philosophizing must be infectious.

Socrates: What do you want to talk about?

Peter: Something my friend Felicia Flake said today. When I tell you about it, you'll think I've been talking to a first-rate fool.

Socrates: I would expect so. She is a daughter of Eve, just as we are sons of Adam.

Peter: You mean you think we're fools too?

Socrates: Don't you?

Peter: Not like Felicia.

Socrates: Because she's a first-rate fool?

Peter: Yes.

Socrates: Is that better or worse than a second-rate fool?

Peter: Much worse.

Socrates: Are you sure?

Peter: Sure.

Socrates: And are you quite sure which of you is the first-rate fool and which the second-rate fool?

Peter: Are you insulting me?

Socrates: Nothing personal, Peter. It's just that there are so very few things I am sure of, but one of the few things I know is that everyone is either a first-rate fool or a second-rate fool.

Peter: How do you figure that?

Socrates: The world, it seems to me, is divided into the wise, who know they are fools, and the fools, who think they are wise.

Peter: Well, Felicia is certainly one of the fools.

Socrates: Why? What is her foolishness?

Peter: Superstition, Socrates, superstition. Surely you are suspicious of superstition.

Socrates: I might be suspicious of it if I knew what it was. But since I do not, I can only be suspicious of thinking I know what it is when I do not.

Peter: You don't know what superstition is?

Socrates: No. Do you?

Peter: Oh, no you don't. I'm onto you by now. I'm not going to let myself be tricked into that trap again.

Socrates: So you *don't* know what superstition is?

Peter: No.

Socrates: And yet you call your friend a fool because of it? Do you think that is a wise thing to do, or a foolish thing?

Peter: O.K., so I do know.

Socrates: Then would you please tell me?

Peter: No, I don't know what it is. So I take it back—what I said about Felicia.

Socrates: Then since you now do not know what superstition is, the thing to do would be to find out, wouldn't it?

Peter: You've got me either way, Socrates.

Socrates: Will you search with me for a definition of this thing?

Peter: Oh, all right. But you mean a definition of the *term*, don't you?

Socrates: No, I mean a definition of the *thing*. Superstitions are real things, aren't they?

Peter: Of course not. They're illusions. That's why we call them superstitions.

Socrates: So you *do* know what superstitions are. But there is a confusion here. The object believed in by the superstition may be illusory rather than real; but the superstitious *belief* in that object is a real occurrence in the mind of the believer, is it not?

Peter: Oh, of course. In that sense even superstitions are real.

Socrates: And we should define real things and not just words, shouldn't we?

Peter: I suppose so, but I don't see the importance of that distinction.

Socrates: If we define only words, nothing checks us and brings us up short, and we can never be wrong or in error, since we make all the words, and we can make them as we choose. But we do not make all the real things in the world, and these things can be the standards for our definitions. Unlike words, things remain the same no matter what we say. Thus they can make some of our definitions right and others wrong: those that tell us how things really are in the world are right and those that do not are wrong. Do you see the distinction? I believe logicians call it the distinction between nominal definitions and real definitions.

Peter: I see that. But frankly, Socrates, I'm bored already with all this logic. I have something very interesting to talk about today—Felicia's superstition—and you have already turned our conversation around to one of the most boring questions in the world. Frankly, I don't care what a definition is, or even what the real definition of superstition is. What I care about is Felicia's superstition. Can we talk about that, please?

Socrates: As you please. But I can't guarantee that talk about logic may not push its way up out of the deep and into our talk, like the Loch Ness monster.

Peter: How did you know that was what I wanted to talk about?

Socrates: What? Logic?

Peter: No, the Loch Ness monster.

Socrates: I just used the Loch Ness monster to symbolize logic.

Peter: But that's Felicia's superstition.

Socrates: What? Logic?

Peter: No, the Loch Ness monster! Did Felicia talk to you about it?

Socrates: No.

Peter: Then you must have read my mind. But no, that can't be. That's another superstition.

Socrates: How do you know that either of the two is a superstition if you don't know what a superstition is?

Peter: I refuse to be swallowed by your logic monster.

Socrates: That is hardly a refutation. Or even an answer.

Peter: Just let me tell you some of the other things Felicia believes, and you decide whether she's a superstitious fool or not. She believes in flying saucers, too, and Bigfoot. What do you think of that?

Socrates: What do *you* think?

Peter: I think it's ridiculous. Almost as ridiculous as believing in the Tooth Fairy, or the Easter Bunny, or Santa Claus.

Socrates: What! You mean you don't believe in Santa Claus?

Peter: You're kidding... aren't you?

Socrates: What do you think?

Peter: I never know with you.

Socrates: Neither do I.

Peter: You mean you don't know whether you believe in Santa Claus?

Socrates: I mean I don't know whether I *should* believe in Santa Claus. I'm not sure whether he exists or not. Are you?

Peter: You're not kidding, are you?

Socrates: No.

Peter: Oh, come on, Socrates. It's silly enough to believe in flying saucers and the Loch Ness monster. But to believe in Santa Claus at your age ... how old are you, anyway?

Socrates: Two thousand four hundred fifty three years old last month. You should have seen my birthday cake. Do you know how many angels can dance on the head of a single candle?

Peter: Socrates, get serious. Act your age.

Socrates: What does my age have to do with it, anyway?

Peter: No one over twelve believes in Santa Claus.

Socrates: I didn't say I believed in Santa Claus. I said I didn't know.

Peter: Why are you looking around so furtively?

Socrates: To be sure no child under twelve overheard us.

Peter: Socrates, be serious. This is a university.

Socrates: I know. I invented them.

Peter: Well, a university is devoted to knowledge, not superstition.

Socrates: There goes that word again. We've not been able to catch it yet; it flies past so quickly. May I ask you one little question?

Peter: All right, but not about definitions.

Socrates: How do you know there is no Santa Claus?

Peter: You are serious, aren't you?

Socrates: I told you I am.

Peter: Well, if there was a Santa Claus, why hasn't he been photographed?

Socrates: Oh, but he has. Many times. Haven't you ever seen any pictures of him? There must be millions of them.

Peter: But those are all photos of ordinary people dressed in Santa suits.

Socrates: How do you know that? Have you investigated every one?

Peter: You mean you think the real Santa sneaked into Macy's one night?

Socrates: No, I mean just what I said: how can you be sure?

Peter: Well, why don't we see him the rest of the year?

Socrates: How do you know you don't? Would you recognize him without his red suit?

Peter: Where is he now, then?

Socrates: How should I know? The world is a very big place, you know. I suppose he is at home.

Peter: At the North Pole?

Socrates: Perhaps.

Peter: Then why haven't any cameras photographed him there?

Socrates: Even the vicinity of the North Pole is a big place, is it not? Perhaps the few cameras near there just never got near enough.

Peter: How could he live way up at the North Pole?

Socrates: Do effective heating systems exist, or not?

Peter: Well, how could his reindeer fly through the air? Got you there!

Socrates: Why, by magic, of course.

Peter: Oh, come on, now!

Socrates: Is that a new logical refutation I haven't heard about yet?

Peter: Prove to me there is real magic.

Socrates: No, you must prove to me there isn't. You are the one who claims to be sure, remember? I am a Santa agnostic; you are the Santa atheist. And your "proof" that there is no Santa assumes that there is no magic. So I rightly demand of you that you prove your assumption. How do you know there is no magic?

Peter: That's not fair. All I wanted to do today was to tell you about Felicia's silly superstitions, and now you come out with an even sillier one.

Socrates: You call my agnosticism a superstition?

Peter: Here we go again.

Socrates: I know we haven't defined the term yet, but don't we usually use it to refer to some sort of belief that is unwarranted?

Peter: Yes.

Socrates: But I have no belief in Santa, nor unbelief. I think it is *you* who are superstitious, for you claim to know something that you seem not to have warrant for.

Peter: I *don't* believe.

Socrates: You believe in something that does not exist.

Peter: What?

Socrates: Your so-called knowledge that there is no Santa Claus. I do not think you really have such a knowledge.

Peter: Why not?

Socrates: Because a claim to such a knowledge is more than a mortal can have. I think you are claiming a kind of knowledge only a god can have.

Peter: What? Just because I don't believe in Santa Claus?

Socrates: No, because you claim to *know* there is no Santa Claus.

Peter: Why?

Socrates: Consider what you are claiming to know. "There is no Santa Claus"—that is what logicians call a universal negative proposition.

Peter: Oh, oh. Here we go again, into logic.

Socrates: We are immersed in it whenever we speak. I just try to bring it to light, like an x ray. It's quite painless, I assure you.

Peter: Well, I'm an agnostic about that assurance of yours.

Socrates: You know what a proposition is, don't you?

Peter: I think so. A statement. A declarative sentence.

Socrates: Correct. And what then is a universal proposition?

Peter: You tell me. I never had logic.

Socrates: All right. A universal proposition is one like "All men are mortal" or "All swans are white" or "No angels have tails."

Peter: I see.

Socrates: Now every declarative sentence, or proposition, has two terms: subject and predicate. Do you understand that?

Peter: Well, sure. I had twelve years of English.

Socrates: Now how much of its subject term does a universal proposition claim to know?

Peter: All, I guess. That's why it says "*All* men are mortal."

Socrates: Correct again. See how painless logic is?

Peter: Do you doubt that we can know that all men are mortal?

Socrates: Perhaps some other day we can talk about how we know we are all mortal, if life is long enough. But we have not yet examined the other half of a proposition, the predicate. A proposition can be either affirmative or negative, depending on whether it affirms or denies its predicate of its subject. For instance, "All men are mortal" is affirmative, but "No angels have tails" is negative. Do you understand so far?

Peter: Of course. This is easy.

Socrates: But now comes a more difficult point. A negative proposition claims to know about all of its predicate, but an affirmative proposition claims to know about only some of its predicate. Do you see why?

Peter: No. Good grief, how far we are from Santa Claus.

Socrates: But we are not far from our topic, which was not Santa but reasons to believe or disbelieve in him. Look here: affirmative propositions *in*clude the subject class in the predicate class, rather like inserting a smaller container into a larger one. For instance, "All men are mortal" includes all men in the larger class of mortals. Clear so far?

Peter: Yes.

Socrates: Now when you include one class in another, you include the smaller class in only a part of the larger one.

Peter: Right.

Socrates: So "All men are mortal" means "All men are some of the mortals there are." So an affirmative proposition claims to know only *some* of its predicate class.

Peter: I see.

Socrates: But negative propositions *ex*clude the subject from the predicate. "No angels have tails" means angels are not in the class of things with tails.

Peter: I see. You include in a part, you exclude from a whole.

Socrates: So a negative proposition claims to know how much of its predicate class?

Peter: All of it.

Socrates: And a universal proposition claims to know how much of its subject class?

Peter: All of it.

Socrates: So a universal negative proposition claims universal knowledge of both subject and predicate.

Peter: Yes. So what?

Socrates: What kind of proposition is this: "There is no Santa Claus."

Peter: I guess it's a universal negative proposition.

Socrates: You're right. So it claims universal knowledge of its subject and its predicate, doesn't it?

Peter: Yes. But I don't see what you're getting at.

Socrates: What is the subject?

Peter: Santa Claus.

Socrates: And what is the predicate?

Peter: I don't know.

Socrates: You mean to exclude Santa from what class?

Peter: I can't tell.

Socrates: Do you mean to say Santa is not a bear?

Peter: No, I mean to say Santa is not real.

Socrates: So your predicate class is "real things," or reality. "There is no Santa" means "Santa is not real," doesn't it?

Peter: Yes.

Socrates: And this is a universal negative proposition?

Peter: Yes.

Socrates: And how much knowledge of its predicate does a universal negative proposition claim?

Peter: All of it.

Socrates: So you claim to know all reality.

Peter: Oops.

Socrates: That was the shortest act of contrition I ever heard.

Peter: I didn't mean to claim that.

Socrates: I should hope not. For consider this: What is the term for "knowledge of all reality"?

Peter: Omniscience, isn't it?

Socrates: Yes. And is this attribute found in any mortal?

Peter: No.

Socrates: In whom, then?

Peter: In God, I guess, if there is a God.

Socrates: So you are implicitly claiming to be God when you claim to know there is no Santa anywhere, in all of reality. I suppose you have searched out every corner of reality so that you can be quite sure Santa is not lurking somewhere? What awe I ought to have toward the mighty mind standing before me if this is so!

Peter: Now I know you're kidding, Socrates. I think I get your point, but could you make it simpler? Without the logic lesson?

Socrates: I will try. Suppose you tell me there is a spider in this room. You need to know only a tiny part of the room to know there is a spider in it, for instance, the seat of this chair.

Peter: Oooh! It's a daddy longlegs!

Socrates: It is quite harmless, I assure you. Now if you tell me there is *no* spider in this room, you need to know every nook and cranny of the room to be sure that is true, don't you?

Peter: Yes.

Socrates: But when you say there is no Santa, your room (so to speak) is the whole universe. So you are claiming knowledge of the whole universe, which only God can have. So you must either give up your claim to know that there certainly is no Santa Claus, or else admit your divine identity and receive my due worship—but what a wonderful earthly disguise you wear!

Peter: I am not God, Socrates, that much I know. I don't believe anyone is.

Socrates: You mean you don't believe in God either?

Peter: No, I don't. I think God is just a great big Santa Claus.

Socrates: So you know there is no God?

Peter: Yes.

Socrates: In that case, there must be a God.

Peter: What? What strange logic is this?

Socrates: Only the logic we both have already admitted. Knowing there is no God is like knowing there is no Santa Claus. It implicitly claims omniscience. Didn't we just go through that little logic lesson?

Peter: Yes. But how does that prove there is a God?

Socrates: Omniscience is divine knowledge, isn't it?

Peter: Yes...

Socrates: How can there be divine knowledge without a divine knower?

Peter: Oh.

Socrates: So for you to know there is no God, you must be God.

Peter: Oops again.

Socrates: Perhaps that is the most profound thing you have said all day.

Peter: Socrates, I'll have to take that one home and think about it.

Socrates: An excellent idea for one who lacks omniscience.

6 On Success and the Greatest Good

Peter: Socrates! Socrates!

Socrates: Why do you run after me so desperately, Peter?

Peter: Because I'm in a desperate state. I just *have* to find out what I want in life, and I have to find out today.

Socrates: You are becoming more of a philosopher each day, Peter, but also more impatient.

Peter: Is that bad?

Socrates: The passion for truth—how could that be bad? But the twenty-four-hour time span you insist on . . . are you serious?

Peter: Yes. I hope you have a lot of time today to talk.

Socrates: I have more time than you can imagine.

Peter: I don't even seem to know what I want anymore.

Socrates: I think you have already found one of the things you want.

Peter: What's that?

Socrates: You want to find out what you want.

Peter: Yes. When I first met you I was only asking what career I should choose. Now I'm asking what I really want *in* whatever career I choose, what I'm really looking for, what my scale of values is. That seems to be the most basic question of all.

Socrates: It is, on a practical level. Philosophers sometimes call it the question of the *summum bonum*, or the greatest good. What is at the top of your scale of values? What is the standard for the whole scale?

Peter: That's the question, all right. I think it's the same question as the question of success. I've always wanted to be successful, but now I'm not sure I know what success means. I used to think about different means to the end of success, but now I have to think about the end itself. Is that the same question, Socrates? It feels like it.

Socrates: I think it is. But let's see whether we can bolster your feeling with understanding. You know what success in repairing a shoe is, don't you?

Peter: Yes.

Socrates: And success in poker?

Peter: Yes.

Socrates: And success in getting high grades?

Peter: Yes.

Socrates: And now you're asking what is success in life as a whole, the thing we all have in common all the time.

Peter: Exactly.

Socrates: So your thoughts have risen to the level of the universal.

Peter: It's also the personal, I think. It's not only the good life and the successful life but the happy life I'm after. I think those three things are just three different ways of saying the same thing. Do you think so too?

Socrates: I do. And here is a clue that we are right: all three are equally universal, are they not? Everyone seeks what seems to be good, or attractive, or desirable. And everyone seeks to succeed at whatever they do. And everyone seeks happiness.

Peter: So what *is* success, or the greatest good, or happiness?

Socrates: I think you know me well enough by now not to expect me to answer you in any other way than with questions, Peter. And I think you know yourself well enough by now to realize that you must pursue this elusive and precious quarry yourself, if you ever hope to find it. I can only be your companion, perhaps your guide, but never your substitute.

Peter: I realize that.

Socrates: Have you done any hard thinking about it?

Peter: Yes, I have. And I came up with a list of five things—candidates, so to speak. Can you help me examine them, and see which one fits the position of president of my life?

Socrates: Life examiner—that's my thing, you might say.

Peter: Well, the first one on my list is money. Somehow that doesn't seem to be as good an answer anymore as it used to, but I'm not sure why.

Socrates: Perhaps we can find out by first examining why it once seemed so attractive to you.

Peter: O.K. Well, it seems pretty simple. Everybody wants it. Everybody pursues it. It's universal, like happiness.

Socrates: And therefore it *is* happiness?

Peter: I guess that's a logical fallacy, isn't it, confusing likeness with identity? But it looked like a good clue: everybody wants it.

Socrates: It is a clue, indeed, and perhaps that's why so many follow it. But it is not a proof. To argue that everyone wants money and everyone wants happiness, therefore happiness is money, is like arguing that everyone wants to eat and everyone wants to drink, therefore to eat is to drink. Logicians call that the fallacy of undistributed middle.

Peter: I can see you aren't addicted to that fallacy.

Socrates: How can you see that?

Peter: Your middle is quite well distributed, under your sash.

Socrates: Thank you. In my time, you know, being fat was envied. Only the rich could afford fat foods. But back to our examination. Tell me, who is the judge of good taste in food and drink? One whose sense of taste is in good order, or one who is starving or alcoholic?

Peter: The former, of course.

Socrates: And who is the judge of good taste in life? The wise or the foolish?

Peter: The wise, of course.

Socrates: Then we should not be led by fools into the pursuit of riches. We won't find the *summum bonum* just by taking polls, will we?

Peter: But the pursuit of riches is not just foolishness, Socrates.

Socrates: Good for you; you're talking back. Why isn't it?

Peter: Money is the way to get whatever you want. It seems to be a sort of skeleton key to all the different doors of happiness. Happiness is "different things to different people" but money is the guarantee of getting them all. That's why it was invented. Do you see the point?

Socrates: Indeed. Money gives you at one stroke whatever money can buy. But how can it give you whatever money can't buy? Are you sure there are no such things? Aren't you in fact seeking one of them right now?

Peter: What thing?

Socrates: Wisdom. The knowledge of what is really valuable.

Peter: Oh.

Socrates: And that can't be bought.

Peter: The philosophy department doesn't seem to think so. Have you seen the latest tuition hike?

Socrates: Perhaps they are not true philosophers, but mercenaries.

Peter: Well, I'm glad you're not a mercenary, at any rate, because I can't afford to pay you. Thanks for the free wisdom.

Socrates: But I have given you no wisdom. You have given it to yourself. All I have done is ask you questions. The assumption of all questioning is that the one questioned has the answer, or can find it. I have only prodded you to discover your own wisdom, not mine.

Peter: But I haven't found any yet.

Socrates: Ah, but you have. That very realization is the first step in wisdom.

Peter: How can wisdom be so negative?

Socrates: Isn't liberation from illusion negative? But isn't it wisdom? If it is an illusion that riches make for happiness, and if cross-examining the claims of riches dispels that illusion, then even if you don't yet know what happiness *is*, you are wiser than before because you now know at least what happiness isn't, and you are freed from your illusion.

Peter: But how can I find out what it *is*?

Socrates: Perhaps we can back into that, so to speak, if we can eliminate all the things it isn't. Like a sculptor, who simply chips away all the pieces of marble that *aren't* a man, and is left with a man.

Peter: But you didn't chip away riches yet. You refuted my two *arguments* for it, but you didn't refute *it*.

Socrates: That is correct. I'm glad to see you're making such progress in logic. Well, then, here is what seems to me a good refutation of riches. See what you think of it. You said happiness was your end rather than a means to some further end, didn't you?

Peter: Yes.

Socrates: But money is only a means to further ends, isn't it?

Peter: Yes, but those further ends are all the things it can buy. That's what I meant by money, not the paper dollars. That's what I thought could make me happy.

Socrates: I see. The ancients called that the distinction between artificial wealth and natural wealth—essentially, the distinction between money and things it can buy. Well, now, natural wealth consists of things like food and drink and clothing and cars and houses, doesn't it?

Peter: Yes.

Socrates: And didn't we admit the other day when we were talking about education and jobs that these things too—your "piece of the pie"—are sought only as means to further ends?

Peter: Yes.

Socrates: Then they cannot be happiness, which is the final end, can they?

Peter: I guess not.

Socrates: Furthermore, you do not desire only a finite, specified amount of happiness, do you?

Peter: No. Who does?

Socrates: But the desire for natural wealth is finite. You can use only so much food, only so many houses, and so forth.

Peter: I see. They don't match, then—happiness and natural wealth. But the desire for artificial wealth isn't finite. I always want more money, just as I always want more happiness.

Socrates: True. But money is good only as a means to buy things, remember? If the things aren't your final end, but only means, how could money be your final end? That's only a means to the means.

Peter: I guess we've eliminated money then. Well, let's look at my second candidate. I was attracted to technology because it gave me power over nature. Maybe it's power that will make me happy.

Socrates: Do you have any reasons for thinking so?

Peter: Well, power seems to be a sort of divine thing. You know, "Almighty God"—power is almost his first name.

Socrates: I thought you didn't believe in God.

Peter: I don't know whether I do or not. But if there is a God, he's got to be all-powerful, doesn't he?

Socrates: Perhaps we can talk about that some other day. It seems like a pretty important question. But suppose there were two gods, one perfect in power but imperfect in goodness, and the other perfect in goodness but imperfect in power. Which one would you seek?

Peter: The good one.

Socrates: Then it is not power that you seek.

Peter: Oh. But happiness *is* being like God, isn't it?

Socrates: And if there is a God, he is both all good *and* all powerful, isn't he?

Peter: I guess so. That's what people mean by "God."

Socrates: Then he cannot use his power for evil, can he, if he is perfectly good?

Peter: No.

Socrates: But we can, can't we?

Peter: Yes.

Socrates: So if happiness is being like God, it must be goodness as well as power.

Peter: I guess so.

Socrates: Here is another way to look at it: you don't think of happiness as evil, do you?

Peter: Of course not. It's the greatest good.

Socrates: But power can be evil.

Peter: Yes.

Socrates: Then happiness cannot be power.

Peter: That was short and sweet.

Socrates: And here is another argument. Isn't power a means, like money? Whereas happiness is an end.

Peter: Enough, already. So it's not power. Let's try my third candidate. I want people to like me. I want to be respected and loved and honored. In fact, I want to be famous. Glory. Isn't that divine too?—the glory of God and all that sort of thing? Honor and glory, that's what I want. And isn't honor the reward for goodness? Even goodness seems to be not the final end, but a means: we want to be good in order to be rewarded, whether by our parents, or our friends, or our society, or by God. "Well done; I'm proud of you"—isn't that what we work for? Don't we even attain a kind of immortality that way, if we get enough honor to make us famous?

Socrates: It seems you have three arguments there.

Peter: I do?

Socrates: Yes. You argued that honor is happiness because it is godlike, the reward of goodness, and the way to immortality. Shall we examine each of these three arguments?

Peter: Yes, let's.

Socrates: First, then, does God's honor *make* God honorable, or good, or divine? Or is the honor paid to God because God is first of all honorable, or good, or divine?

Peter: The latter.

Socrates: Then it is not honor that is the greatest good, but honor is like a grade for a course: an index of a good already there. That good is the cause of the honor, not the honor the cause of the good. So the nature of that good still remains to be found.

Peter: I see. Riches is only a means to the end, and honor is only a result of it.

Socrates: Exactly.

Peter: No. Wait. Perhaps the good is a means to honor, and honor is the end. That was my second argument, I think.

Socrates: Let's look at it, then. Suppose you could receive honor from people by fooling them—not that you really had in you any good or virtue worthy of honor, but you received it anyway. Would that make you happy?

Peter: Not completely.

Socrates: What else do you want? You want to deserve the honor, don't you?

Peter: Yes.

Socrates: And do you want to be honored by the wise or by the foolish?

Peter: The wise, of course.

Socrates: Why? Because you want to deserve it, don't you?

Peter: Yes.

Socrates: So you want to be honorable, not just honored.

Peter: Yes.

Socrates: So it is not honor you want, but honorability—whatever makes you deserve to be honored. And we haven't found what that is yet, have we?

Peter: I guess not.

Socrates: Finally, your third argument also seems weak, for no honor or fame really gives *you* immortality, even if you become one of the very few who are never forgotten, only your *name*. If you're not alive to enjoy your post-mortem fame, how can it bring you happiness?

Peter: It brings me happiness now to look forward to it. It makes dying a little easier to think you left behind something worthwhile.

Socrates: Something really worthwhile or only apparently?

Peter: Really.

Socrates: So here, too, it is not just honor but honorability that you seek.

Peter: I guess it is. So what could that be?

Socrates: That is the question you must ask yourself.

Peter: O.K. I've decided that money, power and glory are not the things I should seek, so there must be something else. I asked my father, and he gave me my fourth answer. Can we look at it now?

Socrates: Of course.

Peter: My father is wiser than I am, I think—more experienced in life, anyway—and he said, "If you only have your health, you have everything." Maybe that's the most important ingredient in happiness.

Socrates: Do *you* think so?

Peter: Maybe.

Socrates: Do you have any reasons other than your father's experience?

Peter: Yes. If it's taken away, we give anything to get it back.

Socrates: That is a reason. But tell me, would you rather suffer a disease of the body or of the mind? Paralysis, for instance. If you had to lose either your health or your sanity, which would you prefer?

Peter: To lose my health, I guess. Say, that's strange.

Socrates: What?

Peter: I always thought of myself as a realistic sort of fellow. All this idealism about the soul being more important than the body—I thought that was just for philosophers and saints. But here I am making the same value judgment.

Socrates: I think we all would make that same judgment. Whether you call it soul, mind, psyche or personality, it's your very self. And you want *that* healthy and happy above all, don't you?

Peter: Yes. But I had thought that my self was my body.

Socrates: If your body is simply you, why do you call it *your* body?

Peter: I don't follow you.

Socrates: "Your" is a possessive pronoun, isn't it?

Peter: Yes.

Socrates: And the possessor is more than the possessions he possesses, isn't he?

Peter: Yes.

Socrates: And since you call it "your" body, you claim to possess it. So there must be a *you* more than just your body, to be its possessor, and the possessor of its health.

Peter: I see.

Socrates: And here is a second argument. Would you say that a human being can be happier than any animal, because of his mind, his understanding and appreciation of life?

Peter: I guess I would say that, yes.

Socrates: And would you also agree that in other bodily goods besides health, some animal or other is usually superior to man? For instance, turtles live longer, and tigers are stronger, and eagles are faster.

Peter: Of course. But what does that prove? How can you use the zoo to argue about the greatest good for man?

Socrates: Well, if animals are greater than men in bodily goods and man is greater than any animal in happiness, then happiness can't be a bodily good.

Peter: That does logically follow.

Socrates: But health is a bodily good.

Peter: I see. So health cannot be the essence of happiness. I think I always knew that. My father is a bit of a hypochondriac, and a hypochondriac isn't very happy.

Socrates: Would you like to know the reason? It's another argument against health as the essence of happiness.

Peter: Yes.

Socrates: Suppose you were a ship's captain. You would want to preserve your ship, wouldn't you? To keep it shipshape?

Peter: Of course.

Socrates: You might call that the health of the ship.

Peter: Yes.

Socrates: But would that be your primary concern? Or is it only a means to some further end?

Peter: A means. A healthy ship can carry freight, or passengers, or fight in a navy.

Socrates: So the mere preservation of health is not your end.

Peter: I see. You mean my body is like a boat and my soul is like its captain.

Socrates: Yes. And a captain who is worried above all about the health of his ship and who ignores what his ship is *for* is not a wise captain, is he?

Peter: No.

Socrates: But that is what a hypochondriac is like.

Peter: O.K., it looks like my first four candidates have all gone down the tubes.

Socrates: Yes, and do you see why? Any common deficiency in all of them?

Peter: Why bother reviewing lost causes?

Socrates: Because it may help us to find a cause we will not lose. If we find a common deficiency, then whatever does not have that deficiency is likely to be what you are looking for.

Peter: O.K. Mmmmm... didn't every one of the four turn out to be a means rather than the end? Except honor. But even that was not desired for its own sake alone. I think happiness will have to be something we all want just for the sake of having it, and for nothing else. It would have to be like that if it's the greatest good, the last end. That's why I think it's pleasure. That's my fifth and best answer, I think. It's an end, not a means. Nobody seeks pleasure for the sake of riches, or honor, or power. But people seek those things for the sake of pleasure. And here's a second argument: not everyone seeks honor, or power, or money, but everyone seeks pleasure.

Socrates: Shall we examine your fifth candidate, or elect it without an examination?

Peter: Examine away.

Socrates: Pleasure does seem to be part of the meaning of happiness, which is why we treat it as an end rather than a means. But we still do not know its cause.

Peter: Its cause?

Socrates: Yes. Must not something cause pleasure?

Peter: Yes.

Socrates: What?

Peter: Anything. Whatever turns you on. Different strokes for different folks. Philosophy for you, beer and pretzels for somebody else.

Socrates: So you think happiness may consist in bodily pleasures for some and the pleasures of the mind for others?

Peter: Exactly.

Socrates: I see some problems with that. See whether you can solve them. For one thing, the greatest good must also be the least evil, or the farthest from evil, mustn't it, since good and evil are opposites?

Peter: Yes.

Socrates: But bodily pleasures often coexist with great evils, whether of body or soul. For instance, an unhealthy body can find pleasure in things that make it even more unhealthy—drugs or alcohol, for instance. And the unhealthy soul of a tyrant can find pleasure in his very wickedness.

Peter: That's true.

Socrates: So since bodily pleasures are compatible with evil, and the greatest good is not, physical pleasures cannot be the greatest good.

Peter: Then why are they so satisfying?

Socrates: They aren't! And that's a second reason. Even after you get them, you still lack other things—health, for instance, or power, or wisdom, or a good conscience. But that cannot be true of happiness, the greatest good: as the final end, it must be adequate, and satisfying.

Peter: Oh. That's right.

Socrates: And here is a third reason. Pleasure comes from things in the outside world, doesn't it?

Peter: Yes, but it's in us. It's not a physical thing.

Socrates: But it is caused by physical things.

Peter: Yes.

Socrates: Thus it is subject to fortune, good or bad.

Peter: Yes.

Socrates: Are you happy if you are held hostage?

Peter: Hostage? No. What do you mean?

Socrates: Pleasure is hostage to fortune.

Peter: All right. You're firing off arguments like cannon balls. I guess I'll have to admit that it's something in the soul, then, wisdom or virtue of something like that. All five of my answers were shot down, so I guess we go for answer number six. That's what you had up your sleeve from the beginning, isn't it? Health of soul?

Socrates: I am no magician. I have nothing up my sleeve.

Peter: Well, that's the only answer left, isn't it? If it's not the good of the body, it has to be the good of the soul, doesn't it?

Socrates: Does it?

Peter: What else could it possibly be?

Socrates: Are the soul and the body the only things in all of reality?

Peter: No, but nothing less than ourselves can satisfy us, so it has to be ourselves. It's a big world out there, but in a way it's smaller than us. Inner space is bigger than outer space. So we are our own end, right? "Know thyself" and all that?

Socrates: Shall we examine candidate number six?

Peter: Certainly. But this has to be it. There simply is nothing else.

Socrates: Are you sure?

Peter: I remember I had some problems the other day with that claim.

Socrates: Yes—your universal negative implies universal knowledge. But let's just look at this one thing, virtue, or health of soul. Tell me, can a moving arrow be its own target?

Peter: No, but how is that looking at virtue?

Socrates: Is not the seeking soul like a moving arrow?

Peter: Yes.

Socrates: And the end sought by the seeking cannot be moving, can it?

Peter: Why not?

Socrates: How could we make progress toward it if it were? How can you hope to cross an ever-receding goal line, or steal a moving second base?

Peter: Oh. You mean the soul is in process, but the end is not;

therefore the soul can't be its own end.

Socrates: You put it much more exactly than I.

Peter: But what else is there if we've eliminated the world, the body and the soul?

Socrates: Perhaps we should apply our principles of elimination once again and find out why all these things were deficient. That would give us at least a negative definition of whatever it might be that is not deficient, and thus answer your question.

Peter: All right. Let's see. Nothing we looked at in our six candidates was enough. Nothing was big enough. Everything was a little good, a partial good. Each thing left something else outside, something else to be desired. Isn't that our problem?

Socrates: Again your exactness is impressive. You are becoming quite philosophical.

Peter: So if we ever did find the greatest good, it would have to be total, not partial—universal, not particular. Otherwise, we would still want something more.

Socrates: You are getting warmer.

Peter: It's like thinking. No matter how many thoughts you come up with, you're not finished. You just can't draw a limit to thought and say that after 5000 thoughts, you can't think one more. It seems to be the same with desire. You can't say after a million good things that you don't want one more.

Socrates: In other words, the mind seeks the universal truth, or truth as such, and the desire seeks the universal good, or good as such.

Peter: I guess that's saying the same thing in different words, more abstractly. But then that raises the question: Isn't this universal good just an abstraction? Maybe there isn't any such thing. Maybe that's why we couldn't find it. Maybe it's like greenness, or squareness—just an abstraction. Maybe it's just parceled out through millions of little concrete goods, as greenness is only in green things and squareness in square things. Maybe there is no single concrete universal good.

Socrates: How philosophical you have become!

Peter: But I've run up against a wall with my philosophizing. How can I pursue this question of a concrete universal good? How could there be one single good that is all good?

Socrates: I think this is the point where you must leave me.

Peter: Leave you? But I've just begun.

Socrates: And you have learned Lesson One: that you have just begun. I taught you that, but you will have to learn Lesson Two yourself.

Peter: But where shall I go? You have the words, the way, the questions.

Socrates: If you are in the market for the concrete universal good, you might try the religion department.

Peter: Oh. That's right. God would be a concrete universal, wouldn't he?

Socrates: But I wander in and out of that place frequently too. So you are not finished with me. Not until you reach the very end.

II.
SOCRATES
AND
FELICIA FLAKE

7 On Pot and Happiness

Felicia Flake: Hi, man. Lookin' for a joint?

Socrates: I am neither a butcher nor a surgeon. Why should I be looking for a joint?

Felicia: I mean a roach. You lookin' for a roach?

Socrates: I am not an exterminator either. Do you have a cockroach problem here at Desperate State?

Felicia: Oh, a funnyman! Are you kidding or are you innocent?

Socrates: Neither, I think.

Felicia: You *think*? You don't *know*?

Socrates: You have finally identified my profession. But one thing I do know: I don't know what you are talking about.

Felicia: I'm talking pot, man.

Socrates: What is "potman"?

Felicia: Do you want to smoke some pot with me or not?

Socrates: How do you smoke a pot?

Felicia: Not *a* pot, silly; *pot.*

Socrates: You mean you think you can smoke a universal rather than a particular.

Felicia: Huh?

Socrates: I mean...

Felicia: Never mind. Hey, if you're kidding, you're getting pretty tedious, and if you're not, you must be from another world.

Socrates: In a sense...

Felicia: You really don't know what pot is?

Socrates: No. Will you tell me?

Felicia: Better. I'll give you. Try it; you'll like it.

Socrates: May I know what it is first?

Felicia: You mean you won't try it unless you analyze it first? What kind of a coward are you?

Socrates: Is it cowardly to want to know? Are wisdom and courage exclusive?

Felicia: Oh, now I know what you're doing. You're impersonating a philosopher. Say, you look just like Socrates. I know all about that cat; studied him last year. Are you going to a costume party or something?

Socrates: Something like that. This intellectual smorgasbord called Desperate State University rather resembles a costume party, I think, with all its role-playing guests. But I am not impersonating Socrates; I'm the original.

Felicia: Sure you are. You're pretty original at that. O.K., I'll go along with the gag.

Socrates: Gag? I don't want to gag you, but release you from your cave.

Felicia: And what do you do, O philosopher?

Socrates: I philosophize, of course.

Felicia: O, right. Dumb question. Score one for the little Greek. What next?

Socrates: You were talking about something called "pot." Will you tell me what it is?

Felicia: Sure. It makes you high.

Socrates: Is it a ladder?

Felicia: No, it's a drug.

Socrates: A drug to make me taller? Five feet high is quite enough for me.

Felicia: No, silly, to make you happy.

Socrates: How remarkable! A drug for unhappiness! And do you use this drug a lot?

Felicia: Yes.

Socrates: Then you must be very unhappy, otherwise there would be no need to use it. But if you are unhappy, the drug is not working, so why do you continue to use it?

Felicia: Oh. I don't know. I never thought of it that way.

Socrates: What a fast learner you are!

Felicia: What did I learn?

Socrates: That you do not know. That is Lesson One.

Felicia: Well, tell me Lesson Two then. Tell me why I shouldn't.

Socrates: I do not teach by telling. I teach by asking.

Felicia: Oh, right. The good old "Socratic dialog." You play your part well. O.K., I guess if you won't get stoned with me, I'll have to play it straight with you.

Socrates: Do they stone you for using this drug?

Felicia: It's just an expression.

Socrates: You mean they stone you for an expression?

Felicia: I think we have some communication problems here.

Socrates: I should think so, if they stone you for using certain expressions.

Felicia: I just meant that "stoned" and "straight" were mere words.

Socrates: "*Mere* words"? There is nothing mere about a word, my dear.

Felicia: Felicia's the name. Felicia Flake.

Socrates: How felicitous. Do you mean to say that your words do not mean what they say?

Felicia: Forget it. Let's not talk about words. Let's talk about pot.

Socrates: But how can we talk except in words?

Felicia: Let's just talk pot.

Socrates: I have never seen pots coming from a speaker's mouth, only words.

Felicia: O.K., cut the comedy and quiz me. I'll play my part. What do you want to know?

Socrates: Everything. But one thing at a time. You say "pot" is a drug?

Felicia: Yes.

Socrates: Do not all drugs alter the chemistry of the body in some way?

Felicia: Yes.

Socrates: And is there a state of body chemistry that can be called the natural or healthy state?

Felicia: No, not necessarily. Who's to say what's natural?

Socrates: Doctors. When they prescribe drugs, do they not have this state of health in mind, and do they not select a drug on this basis—what is most likely to return the patient to the state of health?

Felicia: That sounds too simple to me.

Socrates: *Diseases* are far from simple—there are many states called diseases, just as there are many angles at which we can fall. But just as there is only one angle at which we can stand upright, there is one health which is the standard by which we judge the many diseases, is there not?

Felicia: Are you trying to say pot makes me sick?

Socrates: No, I'm trying to say exactly what I said. Shall I repeat it?

Felicia: I know what you're leading up to. But pot makes me feel great.

Socrates: And therefore it gives you health rather than disease?

Felicia: Exactly.

Socrates: You realize the assumed premise of that argument?

Felicia: Yeah, I took logic.

Socrates: Well?

Felicia: I don't know. I forgot most of that stuff.

Socrates: What grade did you get in your logic course?

Felicia: B plus.

Socrates: I see this university is well named. How about this premise—"whatever makes you feel good gives you health."

Felicia: Yeah, that's it.

Socrates: And do you agree with that?

Felicia: Sure.

Socrates: So disease and health are determined by feeling?

Felicia: Yes.

Socrates: But might we not feel fine and be about to die? Or might we not feel in great pain but have only a minor cut or headache?

Felicia: O.K., so health isn't just feeling. But I still say, "If it feels good, do it."

Socrates: Would you torture me if it made you feel good?

Felicia: Aren't you doing just that to me right now?

Socrates: If you answer my question, I'll answer yours.

Felicia: My answer is no.

Socrates: So is mine. Now why wouldn't you torture me?

Felicia: Because it wouldn't make me feel good.

Socrates: But suppose it did?

Felicia: You know, it's beginning to feel better with every question you ask. No, I still wouldn't do it.

Socrates: Why not?

Felicia: I'd be caught, and imprisoned. Bad consequences.

Socrates: And if you know you wouldn't be caught?

Felicia: Still no.

Socrates: Why not?

Felicia: I don't know.

Socrates: Lesson One again. Good for you. And are you sure there are no bad consequences of pot, even if you don't get caught?

Felicia: Sure.

Socrates: How do you know that?

Felicia: I don't know.

Socrates: You don't know *how you know* there are no bad consequences, or you don't know with certainty that there *are* no bad consequences?

Felicia: I know I'm getting impatient with this logic. Look, it's very simple. It makes you high and happy.

Socrates: Could you describe this state?

Felicia: Sure. It's like a good dream. Calm. Relaxing.

Socrates: I see. Tell me, which is more valuable, waking or sleeping?

Felicia: I can't say. It depends.

Socrates: Can you say whether we sleep for the sake of waking or wake for the sake of sleeping?

Felicia: The first, I guess.

Socrates: And an end is more valuable than a means, is it not? A thing worth having for its own sake, like pleasure, is more valuable than a thing which is only a means to it, like money, isn't that so?

Felicia: Yes.

Socrates: Then since we sleep as a means to waking, waking is more valuable.

Felicia: All right, so what?

Socrates: And dreams are part of sleep?

Felicia: Yes.

Socrates: Why then do you exchange waking for dreaming, the more for the less valued state, by taking the drug?

Felicia: Same reason we go to sleep at night: we need it.

Socrates: I see. Wouldn't you be better off if you needed less sleep?

Felicia: No way. I'd be a nervous wreck.

Socrates: No, I don't mean *getting* less sleep even though you need it. I mean not *needing* as much sleep. If you needed sixteen hours sleep a night, wouldn't that be unenviable?

Felicia: Yes.

Socrates: Then if you didn't need the induced sleep of this drug, you would be in a more enviable state.

Felicia: I just know it makes me happy, that's all. And happiness is an enviable state.

Socrates: Do you prize happiness above wisdom, and knowledge, and awareness of reality?

Felicia: Yes. Wisdom can make you pretty unhappy, I think.

Socrates: Do you really think so?

Felicia: Yes.

Socrates: And do you think that thought is a wise one or a foolish one?

Felicia: A wise one. Why would I say something I thought foolish?

Socrates: And did that wise thought of yours make you unhappy?

Felicia: As a matter of fact, yes. It's pretty depressing to think about the unhappiness wisdom brings you.

Socrates: Yet you deliberately entertained this unhappy thought. You preferred it, preferred wisdom to happiness. It seems you do not always practice what you preach.

Felicia: All this logic is giving me a big headache. I need a joint.

Socrates: Do you really need it, or do you only think you do?

Felicia: What difference does it make?

Socrates: If you only think you do, then you are mistaken, and you need to be delivered from your mistaken thought. If you really need it, you are addicted to it, and need to be delivered from your real addiction.

Felicia: I'm not addicted. I can take it or leave it.

Socrates: You don't need it, then?

Felicia: No.

Socrates: A moment ago you said you did.

Felicia: I need it but I'm not addicted to it.

Socrates: What is the difference then between a need and an addiction?

Felicia: I don't know. I never thought about that.

Socrates: Shall we begin?

Felicia: Well, I guess the difference is that I can resist it.

Socrates: Are you sure?

Felicia: Yeah, yeah, I'm sure.

Socrates: Why then are your hands trembling?

Felicia: Look, even if I do need it, it's not bad stuff. It's not as bad as alcohol. There's the real addiction. Do you know how many alcoholics there are in the world? A lot more than pot-heads. And do you know how destructive alcohol makes people? Pot makes you nice; booze makes you nasty. Pot makes you glad, booze makes you mad.

Socrates: What conclusion do you draw from the fact that more people are addicted to alcohol than to pot? That addiction to pot is not an addiction? Or that this addiction is good?

Felicia: It's not the numbers. Pot makes you happy.

Socrates: And therefore it is harmless?

Felicia: Yes.

Socrates: Assuming that everything that makes you happy is harmless?

Felicia: I don't want to argue it. It's just nice, that's all. It makes you nice.

Socrates: Why then does your society make it illegal?

Felicia: Some old squares say it's bad.

Socrates: What reasons do they give?

Felicia: They say it makes you passive, and that it's psychologically addictive, even though it isn't physically addictive, and that it leads to harder drugs that *are* harmful. But there's no hard proof of all that.

Socrates: Is there "hard proof" that "all that" is false?

Felicia: No. The jury is still out.

Socrates: Then why do you court the three dangers you just mentioned?

Felicia: I'm not a coward.

Socrates: Is it cowardice to shun dangers there is no reason to risk?

Felicia: There's reason.

Socrates: Yes?

Felicia: You get your jollies out of analyzing terms; I get mine from this stuff.

Socrates: Happiness, you mean? Felicity?

Felicia: Right on, man.

Socrates: Tell me, does your happiness come from the drug, or from your mind?

Felicia: From the drug. *Yours* comes from your mind.

Socrates: I think yours does, too, and I think I can show that to you. Did you ever hear of the principle of causality?

Felicia: Sure. I took philosophy.

Socrates: Do you agree that an effect cannot be greater than its cause?

Felicia: Of course.

Socrates: Now a drug is physical, is it not?

Felicia: Yes.

Socrates: And whatever is physical is limited to quantity and matter and space, is it not?

Felicia: Yes.

Socrates: And that is less than something that is *not* limited to quantity and matter and space?

Felicia: If it's real, yes. Abstract concepts aren't measurable in quantity and matter and space, but they're not realities.

Socrates: What about consciousness. Is that a reality?

Felicia: It happens, yes.

Socrates: And is it quantifiable? Is it measurable spatially? Does

it have mass?
Felicia: No.
Socrates: Then consciousness is greater than matter.
Felicia: I don't know. How can you say "greater"?
Socrates: Do rocks think?
Felicia: No.
Socrates: Is it greater to be able to think, or not to be able to think?
Felicia: To be able to think.
Socrates: All right, then, consciousness is greater. Now is happiness measurable by quantity and matter and space?
Felicia: No. It's a matter of consciousness.
Socrates: Like thought.
Felicia: Yes.
Socrates: Then how can a merely physical drug give you this more-than-physical effect?
Felicia: Oh, it's just a catalyst.
Socrates: The cause is the mind, then?
Felicia: Yes.
Socrates: So it is your mind that makes you happy.
Felicia: Yes.
Socrates: You are like me, then.
Felicia: There's a difference.
Socrates: Yes, and I think it is this: it is truth that makes me happy, while it is illusion that makes you happy.
Felicia: Different strokes for different folks.
Socrates: You mean happiness is purely subjective, like pleasure, rather than objective, like health?
Felicia: Exactly. Happiness *is* pleasure.
Socrates: I think I can show you that it is not. Tell me, please: what is the opposite of pleasure?
Felicia: Pain.
Socrates: You cannot be in pain and in pleasure at the same time in the same way, can you, if these are opposites?

Felicia: No.

Socrates: Then if happiness is the same as pleasure, no one could ever be happy and in pain at the same time, happy about the very thing that was causing the pain.

Felicia: Exactly.

Socrates: Have you ever heard of growing pains?

Felicia: Sure.

Socrates: Do you think they are ever freely and deliberately chosen?

Felicia: Sometimes.

Socrates: And what is the motive behind every choice we make? Is it not happiness? Do we not seek everything we seek because we think it will lead to happiness?

Felicia: They say, "What good is happiness? It can't buy money."

Socrates: And that saying is humorous only because it reverses the truth. What good is money? It can't buy happiness.

Felicia: That's what I say. What good is anything if it doesn't bring you happiness? And pot brings me happiness.

Socrates: Then we do seek all that we seek for the sake of happiness.

Felicia: Yes.

Socrates: Then sometimes a painful thing makes us happier than a pleasant thing, for sometimes we deliberately seek the painful thing rather than the pleasant thing—like growing pains, for instance, physical or intellectual or emotional.

Felicia: I guess so.

Socrates: Therefore happiness cannot be the same as pleasure.

Felicia: All right, Socrates, give me your answer. Tell me what you mean by happiness.

Socrates: No. I am a teacher, and teaching is not telling, remember?

Felicia: Well, if you don't tell me the answers, I'm just going to leave you and go off and have my joint alone.

Socrates: I see. I hope you realize that your apparent act of blackmail is really not an *act* at all.

Felicia: What do you mean?

Socrates: You want to be passive rather than active. Instead of thinking for yourself you want to listen to me. I think that is like what you want with your drug. Passivity is less painful and demanding, after all.

Felicia: Now you *are* telling me something.

Socrates: Why are you complaining now? I am only doing what you asked me to do. *Commanded* me, rather, with a threat. But I will answer... if you will ask. That is active too.

Felicia: Fine. It's a lot easier to ask than to answer.

Socrates: Is that so? I suppose that's why so many teachers use my Socratic method in class?

Felicia: Actually, I never had any who did. But answer my question now, Socrates.

Socrates: What question?

Felicia: What is happiness?

Socrates: Knowledge of truth.

Felicia: And what's that?

Socrates: What? Knowledge or truth?

Felicia: Truth.

Socrates: That's easy.

Felicia: Easy? "What is truth?" is easy?

Socrates: Certainly. Truth is simply saying what is real, saying of what-is that it is.

Felicia: Oh, is that why you're against pot? Because you think it takes me away from reality?

Socrates: Yes.

Felicia: And so it takes away my knowledge of truth?

Socrates: Yes.

Felicia: And so it takes away happiness?

Socrates: Exactly. I couldn't have formulated the argument better myself.

Felicia: Well, why didn't you just say that in the first place? That's a simple argument.

Socrates: Perhaps because I am not as wise as you think. I suppose you can refute this "simple argument"?

Felicia: Sure.

Socrates: I'm waiting.

Felicia: I thought I was asking and you were answering.

Socrates: Do you have any more questions?

Felicia: No.

Socrates: Well, I do. And I'm still waiting for your answer.

Felicia: You mean refute the argument?

Socrates: Yes.

Felicia: Oh. Well, truth is as truth does, so to speak. "What is truth?" anyway, as the great philosopher asked.

Socrates: I just told you what it was. And it was *not* a great philosopher but a fool who asked that question. It was a great philosopher who answered it—by silence. But I think you do not understand that.

Felicia: Truth is relative. Who's to say what the real world is, anyway? Maybe the world I see in my dreams is the real world, and the world we see now is only a dream.

Socrates: Do you really seriously entertain that contradiction?

Felicia: Contradiction?

Socrates: Certainly. That reality is not real but a dream, and that a dream is not a dream but reality, certainly sounds like a contradiction to me.

Felicia: Forget the words. You're tangling me up in my words. The point is, who's to say which world is more real?

Socrates: *You* are, if you have the courage to think for yourself instead of passively receiving it—whether from me or your dream or your drug. Your skepticism is a very easy philosophy, a very passive philosophy. You never have to answer the question: what is real?

Felicia: Frankly, I don't care much what's real.

Socrates: What do you care about, Felicia?

Felicia: Happiness.

Socrates: And you think the drug makes you happy?

Felicia: Yes.

Socrates: You said before that your own mind made you happy, and the drug was only a catalyst. Do you still think that?

Felicia: Yes.

Socrates: Then the drug releases happiness that is in you already?

Felicia: Exactly.

Socrates: Do you need this drug to release your happiness?

Felicia: Sometimes I do, sometimes I don't. Why do you ask?

Socrates: If you need it, it is an addiction. If not, why use a crutch when you can walk without one?

Felicia: So pot is my addiction and philosophy is yours. What's the difference?

Socrates: The difference is that if we are addicted to wisdom, we are addicted to something greater than ourselves, something we really do need. If you are addicted to anything less than yourself, something you do not need, you are a slave.

Felicia: Oh. That was short and sweet.

Socrates: It wasn't meant to be sweet.

Felicia: And our talk hasn't been short either. Look, Socrates, it's been cool, but I gotta split. You know, nobody ever talked to me like this before. And I think nobody ever will again.

Socrates: Oh, I doubt that.

Felicia: What do you mean?

Socrates: I think we will meet again.

8 On Rock...
and Music

Socrates: Hello, Felicia. I told you we'd meet again. What is that strange device you're wearing today? Is it some sort of medical therapy for your ears?

Felicia: Hi, Socrates. Boy, you *are* out of it! This is my Walkman.

Socrates: It does not seem to be walking. Nor does it seem to be a man.

Felicia: I'm listening.

Socrates: To what?

Felicia: My rock.

Socrates: Oh, dear. Perhaps it is more than medical therapy that you need. You think your rock talks to you?

Felicia: Rock is music, Socrates.

Socrates: You think your rock sings to you? Am I wrong to take its stony silence for granite?

Felicia: Silly! It's not *a* rock; it's rock.

Socrates: The abstract universal essence sings to you?
Felicia: Rock music means music that makes you rock.
Socrates: Oh. Would it make me rock too?
Felicia: Here. See for yourself. Listen.
Socrates [Listening]: Oh. But when will the music begin?
Felicia: That's it.
Socrates: I'm not rocking.
Felicia: What did you hear?
Socrates: Not the Muses, certainly. I would hardly know how to describe it.
Felicia: That was hard rock. Maybe you'd like soft rock better.
Socrates: Are soft rocks thrown less painfully at the ear?
Felicia: You might say that. Here, try this one: it's acid rock. And this one: it's punk rock.
Socrates [Listening]: Felicia, I would like to ask you a question that you might consider very strange.
Felicia: Not from you I wouldn't. Ask away.
Socrates: Have you ever considered the possibility that this . . . this . . .
Felicia: Music.
Socrates: . . . that this sound might do any harm to you?
Felicia: You mean the volume? Nah, I'm used to high decibels.
Socrates: No, I mean the spirit.
Felicia: What in the world are you talking about?
Socrates: You do know that music has a magical power, don't you?
Felicia: No. What do you mean?
Socrates: For once, I shall tell you rather than questioning you, since you seem totally at a loss to understand what I mean. A great variety of spirits come to us on the wings of music, into the deepest recesses of the soul. They come to places where the light of reason has never shone. They come gliding past the gate-keeper, Reason, the censor and judge which patrols the soul's borders.

Felicia: You mean music should be censored by reason?

Socrates: Not what I think *you* mean by "reason"—analysis and calculation—but what I mean by reason—sanity, seeing what is, conformity to Truth. This is the proper gatekeeper of the soul. Music slips past him more effectively than anything else. That is why my pupil Plato wanted the state to censor music.

Felicia: How terrible! No music is pretty dreary.

Socrates: No, no, *censor* does not mean "eliminate." It means "judge," or "discriminate." The state was to monitor music.

Felicia: Still terrible. Why the state?

Socrates: This was to be the ideal state, ruled by true philosophers, wise men and women. They would act as substitute censors, so to speak. For the individual has no inner censor against the power of music, as we have against the power of words. I do not say I agree that the state ought to do this job, but I do agree with the psychology here. Music is more powerful than reason in the soul. That is also why Plato made music the very first step in his long educational curriculum: good music was to create the harmony of soul that would be a ripe field for the higher harmony of reason to take root in later. And that is also why he said that the decay of the ideal state would begin with a decay in music. In fact, one of your obscure modern scholars has shown that social and political revolutions have usually been preceded by musical revolutions, and why another sage said, "Let me write the songs of a nation and I care not who writes its laws." But look here! You seem utterly astonished, as if you have never heard anything like this before.

Felicia: I certainly haven't.

Socrates: Then I suppose you also have not heard that it was in music that the worlds were created? Or that music was the original language, the language of the gods?

Felicia: No.

Socrates: What did you think music was?

Felicia: I guess I thought it was to sing words to, and later it became separated from words. Wasn't the first music ornamented words?

Socrates: No. The first music was the language of creation. Poetry came next, then prose. Poetry is fallen music, and prose is fallen poetry.

Felicia: I thought poetry was ornamented prose and music was ornamented poetry.

Socrates: Exactly the reverse. It seems the Great Lore has been forgotten among you. I understand now.

Felicia: Understand what?

Socrates: If the sounds I just heard are typical, I understand why your music sounds more like an attack on the Muses than an inspiration from them.

Felicia: Well! Your point of view is certainly very interesting . . .

Socrates: I have noticed that when you polite people want to offer an insult you often mask it in the meaningless compliment of "very interesting." Please just get to the insult, so that we can argue about the issue. Insults do not threaten me at all, you know.

Felicia: I know. Well, to be quite honest, I think nobody but a few kooks could possibly take what you say seriously today.

Socrates: Oh? Did I forget what day it is today? Is it some special unholy holiday?

Felicia: I mean this generation. We just don't dig your Muses.

Socrates: Has this generation proved that the Muses do not exist?

Felicia: Proved it? No . . .

Socrates: Or that music does not touch the deepest core of the defenseless soul?

Felicia: We know that. We call that the unconscious. Freud discovered it.

Socrates: I see you have never read my pupil Plato's *Republic*. In Book Nine he anticipated Freud's major discoveries some two millennia earlier.

Felicia: I don't care about Freud and Plato. And I don't even care about the Muses, or whether music is magical or not. What I care about is your moralism. I think it's just plain silly to say some music is bad, or harmful—whether rock or anything else.

Socrates: It's silly because it's moralizing?

Felicia: Yes.

Socrates: Do you have some objection to moralizing? Is talking about morality so disreputable to you that anyone who does it is simply disqualified by an epithet, no matter what he says?

Felicia: Morality's O.K. in its place. But not in music.

Socrates: I see. You want to separate morality and music.

Felicia: Yes.

Socrates: Don't you know they are two forms of the same thing?

Felicia: No. What thing?

Socrates: Justice. Harmony. Balance. "Nothing to excess." It was one of the two inscriptions on the temples of Apollo, and the means to the other one, "know thyself." Have you no oracles to tell you these things?

Felicia: I don't know what you're talking about. I just don't see your point about censorship. If music is from the gods, it's good, right? So why censor it?

Socrates: If it is from the gods, it has great power, and we can twist that good power toward great evil. *Corruptio optimi pessima*, you know. Or have you forgotten your Latin moralists too?

Felicia: I never took Latin. Please translate.

Socrates: "The corruption of the best things are the worst things." Or, "The best, when corrupted, become the worst." As one of your English poets has said, "Lilies that fester smell far worse than weeds."

Felicia: I still don't see why you want to censor something good.

Socrates: I think you do see that. I mean, you surely understand why we carefully censor and monitor things that are very good and have great power for good or evil, but we do not bother to censor lesser things. We monitor geniuses, lest they become brilliant criminals, and tigers, lest they become man-eaters, and bombs, lest they explode. But we do not monitor marbles or censor caterpillars or take great care with pebbles. The reason for censoring music is that it carries a power far greater than that of a bomb—a power that touches souls, not just bodies. Thus it touches eternity.

Felicia: Are you one of those religious freaks who says that rock is the Devil's music?

Socrates: I do not know enough about either rock or the Devil to say that. But I am not outraged by that saying in principle, as you seem to be. For if music is a divine thing, it can become a demonic thing. It seems to me that you do an injustice and irreverence to the greatness of music by not allowing that it can ever be evil.

Felicia: How could music be evil? Please explain that.

Socrates: I shall try. What do you think "evil" means, first of all?

Felicia: The opposite of good.

Socrates: And would you say that the greatest good resides in things or in persons?

Felicia: Persons.

Socrates: And within a person, does the greatest good reside in the soul or the body?

Felicia: Gee, I don't know. How could I say?

Socrates: Would you rather have a happy, healthy soul or a happy, healthy body? Do you fear losing your mind or losing your body more?

Felicia: Soul, I guess.

Socrates: And now, what is a good soul? Would you agree with Plato's description of the good soul as the harmonious soul?

Felicia: I've heard of that idea. Yes, I like that.

Socrates: That was not my question. Do you think it is *true*?

Felicia: Yes.

Socrates: And do you think we should judge whether things are good or evil by whether they make people good or evil?

Felicia: Yes.

Socrates: And does music influence the body or the soul?

Felicia: The soul, mainly.

Socrates: Then good music would be music that makes the soul better, that is, more harmonious, and bad music would be music that makes the soul unharmonious.

Felicia: The first part's O.K., but not the second. There's no evil music.

Socrates: But if there is good music, there must be evil music.

Felicia: Maybe there's no good music either, then.

Socrates: Which of the two premises that lead to that conclusion will you deny, then? That music can influence the soul to harmony, or that harmony of soul is good?

Felicia: I don't know. But do you really think the music you heard on my Walkman is *evil*?

Socrates: Perhaps I am untrained in understanding and appreciating it, but it certainly seemed to cause great disharmony of soul in me while I listened to it.

Felicia: Why? Just because it wasn't all sweet and harmonious? Do you think only sweet, nice music is good?

Socrates: Of course not. It is harmony of *soul* we are talking about, not just harmony of musical tone. There is no simple correspondence between the two. And I do not mean by "harmony" merely sweetness. Sweet music, too, can cause disharmony of soul, for instance, weakness, self-pity, or narcissism.

Felicia: What do you mean by harmony then?

Socrates: Justice, right relation, fittingness, appropriateness. You hardly have a word for it in your language. We called it *to kalon:* the-good-and-beautiful, the noble, the fine.

Felicia: So good music isn't just harmonious music.

Socrates: No.

Felicia: Do you think there's one best music for everyone?

Socrates: No indeed. The music appropriate for a soldier would be different from the music appropriate for a poet.

Felicia: Good. Well, rock is appropriate for us.

Socrates: Who is "us"?

Felicia: The young. The alienated. The rebels.

Socrates: I see. I think I understand the music better now; it does seem to express and kindle those feelings. But others as well, less noble ones such as anger and resentment and self-pity and self-importance, if I may trust my emotional antennae. But I wonder why you would want to stimulate these feelings. Or perhaps you think this music exorcises them, like an enema? That was Aristotle's idea, you know: he spoke of a *katharsis*, a spiritual purgation of emotions.

Felicia: You're wandering, Socrates. Stick to the point. What's your question?

Socrates: How logical you are becoming!

Felicia: It's a contagious infection, being around you.

Socrates: Well, I think I mean to ask three questions. First, do you admit that this music expresses these feelings that I have named? Second, do you think these feelings are good for you or bad? Third, do you think this music increases or decreases them?

Felicia: It expresses these feelings, all right, and many others too. It's the music of pure feeling.

Socrates: That's what I was afraid of.

Felicia: But feelings aren't good or evil. They just are.

Socrates: Oh, I think it will be very easy to show you that you don't really think that.

Felicia: Maybe so. But not now, please.

Socrates: All right. And your third answer? Does this music increase these feelings by expressing them?

Felicia: Yes. And that's good because feelings aren't evil.

Socrates: So we must discuss the other question after all.

Felicia: No. We just want to express all our feelings because we're honest, and those are some of our real feelings.

Socrates: Do you mean by "honesty" simply expressing whatever feelings you happen to have at the moment?

Felicia: Sure. Isn't that honesty?

Socrates: A very easy kind. Do you consider this a virtue?

Felicia: Of course honesty is a virtue.

Socrates: But is not every virtue something we are responsible for, something we must choose and work at? How could a virtue be so easy?

Felicia: It's not easy. It costs us.

Socrates: What does this "honesty" cost you?

Felicia: The world scorns us.

Socrates: Is that why rock stars are so rich?

Felicia: Our parents look down on us. Even you call our thing evil.

Socrates: And how great a cost is that? Do you care much for the judgment of us old fogies? Would it not cost much more to be scorned by your peers?

Felicia: Well, what do *you* mean by honesty in feelings?

Socrates: I think honesty with feelings means asking whether they are true.

Felicia: True? How can feelings be true?

Socrates: If I felt passionate love for a stone, would that feeling be true? Or if I felt repulsion when face to face with the face of Helen of Troy, would that feeling be true?

Felicia: I think I see what you mean. Could you put it in a definition?

Socrates: I was right; you are becoming a logician. Well, I should say then that an honest feeling is one that does not lie about its object, one that is appropriate to its object.

Felicia: O.K., now let's apply that to rock.

Socrates: I am at your logical mercy. I think if this music expresses loathing and resentment and scorn at such objects as life, or nature, or work, or reason, or order, or virtue, or authority, or any other great and good thing, then it is not honest.

Felicia: Do you think it does express that?

Socrates: I don't know. It seemed to.

Felicia: Suppose it does. Maybe it's a catharsis after all. If those feelings are bad, as you say, and if rock expresses those feelings, as you say, maybe it's good because it gets them out.

Socrates: In that case you must have a great amount of spiritual waste to eliminate, for this music is very popular, is it not?

Felicia: Yes. So?

Socrates: But you seem to take a quite different attitude toward it than toward waste: a fascination, a sort of fondling.

Felicia: Socrates, you just don't swing.

Socrates: Like a rock. I remain unmoved.

Felicia: And I remain unmoved by your prophetic dooming and damning. We're not decadent, as you imply. We're just into our feelings.

Socrates: Feeling-fondling? Is not auto-eroticism a form of decadence?

Felicia: What is *your* music into, Socrates?

Socrates: If you mean what is it about, it is about its source, the Muses. It is a divine glory.

Felicia: Well, our music comes from us, not from the Muses.

Socrates: I rest my case.

Felicia: What do you mean?

Socrates: That fact itself is evidence of your decadence. For you know neither the heights nor the depths of music, if you think it comes only from you. I seem to see a picture of two castaways on a desert island suddenly receiving a message in a bottle. They feel a sudden hope: news from the real world! Then they read it and their faces fall: they realize that it came only from them. No wonder you do not hear the Muses; your ears are turned inward. And I will hazard a guess that Plato was right in seeing decadence in music as prophetic of all further decadence, for once the most primitive and appealing voice of the gods is subjectivized, other, harder things will follow: you will begin to think that *you* invented society, and civilization, and religion; you will subjectivize right and wrong, and finally even reality itself. Eventually you will believe that the world itself is only a projection of your consciousness.

Felicia: Some of us believe that already.

Socrates: Your philosophers?

Felicia: Some.

Socrates: And your music makers?

Felicia: Some.

Socrates: It fits. The two are only sides of one coin. It's all in our myths, you know.

Felicia: What is?

Socrates: Your history. Have you ever heard of Narcissus?

Felicia: The man who fell in love with his own reflection in the water?

Socrates: Yes. Are not our feelings our own reflections? One could interpret the myth this way: the water in which he drowned was himself. You, too, seem to be drowning in yourselves, if your music is a true index of you.

Felicia: Why do you say that?

Socrates: Does it celebrate anything outside the self and its feelings? Nature, for instance? Or God? Or the true, the good and the beautiful?

Felicia: Sometimes.

Socrates: But not usually.

Felicia: No. But Socrates, you're criticizing not just rock music but nearly all modern art, and modern psychology, and our whole modern lifestyle.

Socrates: Yes.

Felicia: "Yes"? What kind of an answer is that? How can you just sit there blithely and admit that?

Socrates: Are any of these things self-evidently infallible?

Felicia: Nothing is sacred to you, is it?

Socrates: Much is sacred to me. Questioning, for instance. And music.

Felicia: But you're so *negative*!

Socrates: I think I am being positive. To negate a negation is positive, isn't it?

Felicia: Yes . . .

Socrates: So if my critique is true, it is the spirit of your music and your psychology and your society that is negative and lacking and empty. So my critique of it is positive.

Felicia: You've got all the answers, haven't you?

Socrates: No. Just many of the questions.

Felicia: So what do you want me to do? Throw away my rock?

Socrates: Is that impossible? Is it too heavy for you to move?

Felicia: Answer my question.

Socrates: No, I do not ask you to throw away your rock, but to question it, and your psychology, and your society, and your very self.

Felicia: I guess I'll have to think about those things, Socrates.

Socrates: Then our talk has been felicitous indeed.

9 On Sex and Love

Socrates: You seem very happy this morning, Felicia. Have you succeeded in your life's great quest?

Felicia: What quest do you mean?

Socrates: Have you "known thyself" and thus attained felicity?

Felicia: I've attained felicity, all right. But the name of the game isn't knowledge; it's love.

Socrates: I would say those two things are ultimately one. But what kind of love do you mean?

Felicia: The total kind. I just spent an absolutely fabulous night with my boyfriend.

Socrates: That's nice. And what did you do during the night that made you so happy?

Felicia: Stop pretending to be naive, Socrates. We made love, of course.

Socrates: What kind of love did you make?

Felicia: Do you want details? Why, that's none of your business, you dirty old man!

Socrates: I mean, was it *agape* or *philia* or *storge* or *eros*?

Felicia: That's all Greek to me. Speak English.

Socrates: Was it charity, or friendship, or affection, or sex?

Felicia: Charity and friendship and affection are not nighttime loves, Socrates.

Socrates: Oh. I had not realized that the clock limited them so severely. But I think I understand you now. May we bring your nighttime love into the light of day? Or does it fear exposure to the light of reason?

Felicia: Somehow I knew you'd find a way to spoil my fun.

Socrates: If we love a thing, do we not also love to know more about it?

Felicia: Yes.

Socrates: Then you should welcome looking at this thing that you love so much.

Felicia: But it seems so strange to *analyze* love!

Socrates: Why?

Felicia: Because love is like fire, and logic is like a pale light. I don't see how you could add to the light of my fire with your little logic; it's like shining a flashlight on the sun.

Socrates: How can you be sure it's like that until you try? Perhaps there are some dark spots on your sun, and perhaps my logic can x-ray those spots. A sex ray, so to speak.

Felicia: But trying to be logical about sex—it sounds so silly!

Socrates: I thought being silly meant being *il*logical.

Felicia: There's a time and a place for everything.

Socrates: But no time to think about sex? You prefer all heat and no light? A dark fire?

Felicia: My fire has its own light. "The heart has its reasons that the reason does not know," you know.

Socrates: Then let it teach me its reasons. I am willing to learn. Are you willing to help me? Will you share the great good of this mysterious light of yours with me?

Felicia: In words, you mean.

Socrates: Of course. I am much too old for the other thing.

Felicia: How old are you, by the way?

Socrates: Much older than I look, but never too old to learn.

Felicia: Are you too old to have sex anymore?

Socrates: What a silly question! Of course not.

Felicia: I'm curious. How often?

Socrates: Continuously, of course.

Felicia: Wow! You mean continually, don't you? You're resting now, at least.

Socrates: No, I mean continuously. I am male now. My sex is masculine continuously. Does yours change?

Felicia: Oh, *that* "sex." I meant *doing* it.

Socrates: Isn't sex "being it" before it is "doing it"? Do you think sex is only something you do, not something you are?

Felicia: Hmmm. I never thought of that.

Socrates: See? Already you are receiving additional light.

Felicia: Well, what made me happy was doing it. Being it is just ordinary, like a level plain. Doing it was a mountain peak.

Socrates: Then let us inquire about "doing it."

Felicia: What do you want to know? I'm not modest.

Socrates: I can see that. I hope you are not modest in philosophizing. Well, I suppose the first and most important question to ask about anything, once we know *what* it is, is *why* it is. What is its good? Or even, is it good at all, or not?

Felicia: Oh, so you're going to moralize again, are you? Socrates, when are you going to realize that this is the twentieth century?

Socrates: Thank you for that startling piece of news. Do you mean the calendar is your reason for thinking it is good to "have sex" with your boyfriend?

Felicia: I mean everybody's doing it today.

Socrates: I wonder what effect that will have on the world's business and politics in the next twenty-four hours. But seriously, you have given two arguments, it seems . . .

Felicia: I didn't mean to give any.

Socrates: That may be, but logic is our master, not our servant, whether we like it or not. We cannot escape its structures any more than we can escape those of mathematics or physics. You said, first, that it is the twentieth century, and second, that everyone is doing it. If those are your reasons for thinking it is good, then you need a second premise, to the effect that whatever is done in the twentieth century is good, or that whatever everybody does is good, to justify your conclusion. Or is my logical eyesight failing? I seem to see a great gap between your premise and your conclusion, and only one bridge across the gap: the additional premise I just mentioned. Do you spy anything else in the landscape that I have missed?

Felicia: Hmph!

Socrates: You spy a hmph?

Felicia: I spy a hump—a hump in the road that I can't get over.

Socrates: Then you must turn back, unless you can climb over the hump. Can you defend either of those two additional premises of mine that you need, that everything done in the twentieth century is good, or that everything that everybody does is good?

Felicia: Of course not. My argument may be logically weak, but the point isn't logic, it's society. Casual sex is just socially accepted today, as it wasn't in the past. That's what I meant by the twentieth century.

Socrates: It is accepted today. But is everything that is accepted acceptable?

Felicia: Of course; that's what it means. The socially acceptable is whatever society accepts. The acceptable equals the accepted.

Socrates: But does the socially accepted equal the ethically acceptable?

Felicia: How can you distinguish the two?

Socrates: Unless you do, how can you ever make an ethical

criticism of your society? Genocide was accepted in Nazi Germany. Did that make it ethically acceptable, ethically right?

Felicia: No. So what's the distinction, then?

Socrates: The sociological question is: What does society accept? The ethical question is: What is acceptable? The sociological question is: What does society think is good? The ethical question is: What is really good? Do you see the distinction now?

Felicia: Not really. What else can "good" mean outside of society's laws?

Socrates: It must mean something, for if what society thought to be good was always really good, then society would be infallible.

Felicia: Well, *vox populi, vox dei,* they say.

Socrates: I thought you didn't know Latin.

Felicia: Only a few sayings.

Socrates: I think you chose a foolish one here. People are fallible, are they not?

Felicia: Yes.

Socrates: And society is just people, isn't it?

Felicia: Yes.

Socrates: Then society is fallible. But God is infallible. So how could the voice of society be the voice of God?

Felicia: But what becomes of that saying, then?

Socrates: It has been disproved. It's only a saying, after all. You used it as an argument from authority, the weakest of all arguments.

Felicia: Authority? How can the voice of the people be an argument from authority? Authority is the enemy of the people.

Socrates: Surely authority can be the friend of the people? A good policeman, or a lifeguard, for instance?

Felicia: Well, maybe so. But authority is over the people. It's not the voice of the people.

Socrates: In a democracy, it is. Your authority is precisely the voice of the people.

Felicia: I can't believe how you've turned it all around. I thought those who wanted easy sex were the rebels against authority and those who were against it were the ones who always argued from authority.

Socrates: You see now that it is not so. But let us argue not from authority but from reason.

Felicia: Why? Are you anti-authority too?

Socrates: No. But I believe we should have good reasons for believing our authorities.

Felicia: Well, don't you admit that the majority vote is a good reason? If I can get millions on my side and you can get only a few, isn't that a good presumption in my favor, even though it's not infallible?

Socrates: Perhaps. But I do not think you can enlist the majority on your side in this issue of sex.

Felicia: Oh, I've got you there, Socrates. The polls prove it.

Socrates: Do the polls also poll the dead?

Felicia: The dead?

Socrates: If we are to take a vote, let us extend the franchise to the largest class of all. Why insist on the oligarchy of those who happen to be alive now? The dead were people too, and no less wise than the living.

Felicia: You mean past societies would vote against premarital sex? But at least most of the present generation is on my side, and those are the ones we have to deal with.

Socrates: I doubt even that. I think if we took a poll of parents we would get a rather different result from a poll of children. And even from children, I think you would find that most of them wanted their parents, at least, to practice the traditional ethics, including the sex ethics that they want to rebel against. But all this speculation about polls is beside the point, for my authority is not numbers, whether past or present, parents or children, but the authority of the argument. Let us hear your defense of this practice, and we shall examine it by the light of reason.

Felicia: It's the simplest thing in the world, Socrates. It needs no long argument. It just feels good.

Socrates: So your justification is, "If it feels good, do it."

Felicia: Yeah. You got something against pleasure?

Socrates: Indeed not, but I may have something against some pleasant things.

Felicia: I don't dig your distinction.

Socrates: I agree that pleasure as such is good, but not that all pleasant things are good. Do you think they are? A sadist's pleasure, for instance?

Felicia: No.

Socrates: So not everything that is pleasant is good.

Felicia: Maybe not, but most things that are pleasant are good, and this is one of them.

Socrates: Perhaps, but you have still not told me why.

Felicia: Only a nerd would ask that question.

Socrates: What is a "nerd," please?

Felicia: A nerd is someone who doesn't even know what a nerd is.

Socrates: I think we may find some problems with that definition . . .

Felicia: Only if we look. Let's not. The simple point, Socrates, is love. It's love that justifies it.

Socrates: Not just pleasure, then?

Felicia: No, love. Love justifies everything. Love is the meaning of life. Love makes the world go round. Love is the greatest thing in the world. Love is happiness.

Socrates: Ah . . . you will excuse me, I hope, for not immediately sharing your enthusiasm, but I have this strange habit, you see: I want to know what a thing *is* before I declare it to be the greatest thing in the world. So I fear you will have to bear with my tediousness for a while. Now, could you tell me what you mean by love? Is it *eros*?

Felicia: Yes. I told you that already. What's the mystery?

Socrates: What is the *object* of eros?

Felicia: I don't understand.

Socrates: So there *is* some mystery. Let us try to explore it. Is the object of eros your own good, or is it the good of the other person?

Felicia: Are you saying I use him just as a means to my own selfish pleasure?

Socrates: No, I am asking what the object of eros is.

Felicia: I love *him*, so he's the object. Not some abstract "good" but the concrete person.

Socrates: And when you love this person, do you love his body only or also his soul?

Felicia: I don't know what the soul is.

Socrates: Are his feelings important to you?

Felicia: Yes.

Socrates: Are they spatially measurable things?

Felicia: No.

Socrates: But everything in the body is spatially measurable, isn't it?

Felicia: Yes.

Socrates: Then you love his soul too.

Felicia: His feelings, anyway. O.K. So what?

Socrates: And because you love him, you would not want to cause him unhappy feelings, would you?

Felicia: No.

Socrates: Now if he thought you were unfaithful to him, would that cause him unhappy feelings?

Felicia: Yes.

Socrates: So you remain faithful to him?

Felicia: Yes.

Socrates: You have a monogamous marriage, then? Just like an ordinary marriage except for the sanction of state or church?

Felicia: Not exactly.

Socrates: What's the difference?

Felicia: We don't promise to stay together forever.

Socrates: I see. Does the realization that your relationship will probably end some time well before death does you part—perhaps tomorrow—does this fact cause you both any unhappiness?

Felicia: If we think about it, I guess.

Socrates: Then marriage, with its promises, would increase your happiness, wouldn't it?

Felicia: No. We don't believe in marriage. It would box us in.

Socrates: You see the promise of lifelong fidelity as a threat to your happiness?

Felicia: Yes, if and when we fall out of love. We want to be free.

Socrates: Then you do not identify love with happiness, as you said before. For you always want to be happy, but you do not always want to be in this love relationship. Do you identify happiness with freedom, then? You always want to be free—to stay or to leave?

Felicia: I don't know, Socrates. Sometimes I feel drawn to freedom, but sometimes I feel as if I want to be bound. Sometimes I feel so in love with him that I want to get married, even though I don't believe in marriage. It's almost as if love itself wanted to make itself permanent. You'd understand that—as if a god came into me and took over. But then I think: what if I didn't feel this way ten years from now?

Socrates: Is the only love you know a feeling? Something that comes into you and may leave you without your control? Like a god? I wonder who is the primitive, you or I.

Felicia: We identify with the feeling, Socrates, not with laws and promises and duties. They're cold. Love is warm.

Socrates: Yet your love sometimes longs for marriage, with its laws and promises. Perhaps your heart sees what your ideology is blind to.

Felicia: Maybe. But one thing we know: whether we marry or not, it feels right now.

Socrates: "It can't be wrong if it feels so right"?

Felicia: Socrates, you couldn't possibly know what I mean. You're just too old.

Socrates: I suppose the old lose their memories?

Felicia: It's the most beautiful and happy experience of my life. How could something like that be wrong?

Socrates: Your premise, then, is that whatever is beautiful and happy is not wrong?

Felicia: Sure. Don't you think that's true?

Socrates: Suppose I hypnotized you to feel beauty and happiness whenever you stuck pins in me. Would your feeling make it right?

Felicia: No, but that's a silly example. This is not hypnosis.

Socrates: Are you sure?

Felicia: Are you serious?

Socrates: Indeed. Eros is a powerful passion, and our passions often lie to us. If it is as delusive as all the sages have said, its very power would prevent you from seeing through the illusion, just like a powerful hypnosis. No one is so deluded as the one who will not even question whether or not she is deluded. Shouldn't you at least raise the question?

Felicia: It just feels so silly to use logic to pick apart something so beautiful—like a flower.

Socrates: That is exactly how you would feel if you were deluded. No delusion destroys itself. Ask yourself honestly: why are you resisting an objective, logical look at your love? Are you afraid of what you might find?

Felicia: I'll find what I want to find!

Socrates: I see.

Felicia: Oh, I didn't mean that. Or maybe I did; I don't know. Maybe I *was* rationalizing. But how can I know if I'm rationalizing if it's nothing but rationalizing that I'm doing? How can I know if I'm not being honest with myself, if I can't be honest with myself?

Socrates: It is not only rationalizing that you are doing. If you didn't want to be honest with yourself, you wouldn't have asked that question. Your honest part is questioning your rationalizing part, and your rationalizing part is trying to make your honest part feel silly.

Felicia: Are you my honest part, Socrates?

Socrates: No indeed! Do not project onto me your own honesty. Do not do with your honesty what Freud did with conscience: removing it from the individual and locating it without, in society or civilization.

Felicia: No, I won't let you be my honesty, or my conscience. But I don't honestly see why I should have a guilty conscience about making love. The only reason I can imagine is religious authority, and I don't believe in that. You haven't given me any reason for the traditional taboo except tradition itself.

Socrates: It is the same as the reason against divorce, I think. Whether it is a good reason or a poor one, I think I can at least explain it to you. Tell me, do you think marriage is a manmade institution, an artifice, or do you think it is innate, a natural thing, a thing that is discovered rather than invented, made by nature or by God rather than by man?

Felicia: The first, I guess. What difference does it make?

Socrates: If marriage is manmade, it can be man-unmade, like a game. But if it has its own inherent essence and structure and laws, like life itself, then we cannot change them.

Felicia: You mean then we *shouldn't* change them. We do change divorce laws.

Socrates: I mean we *cannot* change them. You cannot change a law of nature, only fight against it. For instance, you can throw a heavy object upward, but that does not change the law of gravity, and the object will eventually fall. Similarly, if there are natural laws inherent in marriage, and if one of these is fidelity for life, then you cannot abrogate that law, though you can work against it rather than with it. But the law remains.

Felicia: Do you mean that when a couple declares a marriage ended, it isn't really ended?

Socrates: Yes.

Felicia: But that's nonsense!

Socrates: Only if marriage is manmade. Only if their choice, their feeling, or their act is the cause of marriage itself. But it is not nonsense if marriage is something bigger than the individuals that ride in it, like an elephant with two fleas on its back.

Felicia: And that's how you traditionalists saw marriage?

Socrates: Yes. And here is a second difference between us. We saw sex as a mystery, a thing whose outer edges seemed full of light and meaning, but whose inner core was full of unknown depths. You tend to see sex as you see everything else: through the bright but narrow slit of science. The very notion of "mystery" is negative and temporary to you: a problem to be solved rather than a glory to be reveled in.

Felicia: Wow! We're farther apart than I thought. It's not just a matter of do's and don'ts, is it?

Socrates: No. And here is a third great difference between us: we ancients saw sex, and marriage, and life itself as a sacred thing, a gift of the gods, a holy and heavenly and high thing, with its head in the sky even as its feet touch the earth. But you use even the phrase "head in the clouds" disparagingly, as if resenting great stature of soul, or heavenly vision. For you, sex is simply earthly: one of the many things on this planet, one of the many things in your life. It is in you, not you in it. It is smaller than you, not greater. It is for you, not you for it. Have I not spoken truly?

Felicia: You have, Socrates. You've clarified the difference between us very well. So you will understand, then, why I do not share your old mysterious taboo.

Socrates: I did not think our conversation would change your mind or your life, but it has finally unearthed three deeper issues on which we differ. Shall we now begin the greater task?

Felicia: What's that?

Socrates: Exploring these issues, of course.

Felicia: Some other day, Socrates. My boyfriend is waiting for me. I think I've had just about all the ancient wisdom I can take today. I guess I'm just a typical modern girl. I want some modern wisdom to take with me. I don't suppose you have any of that?

Socrates: How's this?—Have a nice day, Felicia.

10 On Sexism and Pop Psychology

Felicia: Socrates! What are you doing standing stock still here in the same spot I saw you three hours ago? The sun has moved a quarter of the way across the sky and you haven't moved an inch.

Socrates: I'm waiting. That doesn't require much motion. Also thinking, while I pass the time. That doesn't require much motion either.

Felicia: Who are you waiting for?

Socrates: "Whom."

Felicia: Never heard of him.

Socrates: Have you heard of "Pop" Syke?

Felicia: The resident campus guru? I sure have.

Socrates: Well, he promised to meet me here this morning.

Felicia: Wonderful! He's the greatest man I know.

Socrates: Why is he great?

Felicia: He helps you become great.

Socrates: He sounds great indeed. I suppose it is not your body that he helps to grow?

Felicia: No, the psyche. He's a psychologist.

Socrates: And you? Has he succeeded with you?

Felicia: Oh, yes. Some, anyway.

Socrates: Your psyche guru some, eh?

Felicia: Don't make fun of him, Socrates. A lot of people do, because of his casual style. But he's a beautiful person. Say, what time did he say he'd meet you here?

Socrates: He said first thing this morning. So I came at sunrise. Do you think he has forgotten?

Felicia: No, it's just that he's not a morning person.

Socrates: What a pity—to miss the youth of the day. Almost like missing one's own youth.

Felicia: Oh, here he is now. Pop! There you are!

"Pop" Syke: Hey, man, I'm no magician's rabbit popping out of a hat. Hi, Felicia.

Felicia: Why are you so late?

Pop: I took some soma last night and Old Man Morpheus kept me in bed. The psyche needs its soma, you know; we call it psychosomatic unity.

Felicia: You kept Socrates waiting here three hours.

Pop: Sorry, Soc, I was in the sack. Let me get a better look at you in the light. I only laid eyes on you yesterday for a little blink. Say, you're a real Socrates clone, all right.

Socrates: No, I'm the original.

Pop: Like me, man, like me. One of a kind.

Socrates: I'm afraid we do have at least that in common, yes.

Pop: Never say *afraid,* man. Your fears are between your ears. Psyche out your fears with Pop Syke. Well, what psychic garbage can I flush you two new friends of mine free of today? Shall we have a group grope?

Socrates: I was hoping to ask you a few questions about your work.

Pop: What about Felicia here?

Felicia: If it's all right with you two, I'd like to lay back and listen to this one. I don't get to see two gurus grope every day.

Socrates: Nor will you see it today, Felicia, whatever a "grope" may be, for I am no guru. But you, Pop, what are you? I understand you are a psychoanalyst?

Pop: Nossir! I have declared my independence from the unholy trinity.

Socrates: The unholy trinity?

Pop: Dr. Fraud, Dr. Junk and Dr. Addled.

Socrates: You do not practice any kind of analysis, then?

Pop: Analysis is strictly anal, man.

Socrates: Uh... what is your philosophy, then, if I may ask?

Pop: My philosophy is no philosophy. My only dogma is no dogmas. My golden rule is that there are no golden rules.

Felicia: Isn't he wonderful, Socrates?

Socrates: I don't suppose you ever lose any sleep over contradicting yourself, Pop?

Pop: I don't lose sleep over anything. And I think that's the last thing I'd ever lose sleep over.

Socrates: You *think* so, do you? Then you do think, occasionally?

Pop: I'm a dropout from all schools of thought, man. Feeling's my thing.

Socrates: So I suspected. I don't suppose you'd deign to give any *reasons* for preferring feeling to thought?

Pop: I will if I feel like it.

Socrates: And do you?

Pop: As a matter of fact, yes. Just for you, Soc. Here's one: thoughts divide, but feelings unite.

Socrates: And you want to be a uniter?

Pop: Yup. In fact, my real name is John, and when troubled couples come to me, they say, "Johnny, unite us," and pop! I become a great old quarterback.

Socrates: I see why you are called Pop. It is a kind of corn.

Pop: You're not all grits yourself, man.

Socrates: Are you employed by this university?

Pop: No way, man. This place is positively institutional.

Socrates: Most institutions are, I think. It's not easy for a thing to escape from its own species. But if it's ever done, I wouldn't be surprised that you would be the inventor. Where are you from?

Pop: California.

Socrates: Silly question. What do you do, exactly?

Pop: Nothing *exactly.*

Socrates: Another silly question. I suppose I shall have to settle for what you do inexactly, then.

Pop: I'm a healer.

Socrates: And what do you heal?

Pop: Schism. All kinds of schism, but especially sex schism.

Socrates: Uh-huh. And how do you heal this dread disease of sexism?

Pop: For one thing, I'm planning to rewrite the great textbook of life and remove all the sexist language.

Socrates: The great textbook of life? You mean the Bible?

Pop: No, the genetic code.

Socrates: I see. Nothing like going right to the root of the matter.

Pop: I'm also an inventor and a musician in the Great Cause.

Socrates: And what are you inventing for this cause?

Pop: A new kind of organ.

Socrates: What kind is that?

Pop: A unisex organ.

Socrates: Amazing, the wonders of your modern technology! What else are you doing (though I know it's foolish to ask)?

Pop: Oh, I'm doing lots of composing.

Socrates: Why?

Pop: Because I figure I'll be doing a lot of decomposing in a century or so.

Socrates: I believe that was what they call "a ripe one." Do you follow no psychological theories at all?

Pop: Nope. No nose to the tail for this cat, man.

Socrates: Let me put it another way: how would you classify yourself?

Pop: Don't do it, man. Don't classify me. I'm not a butterfly.

Socrates: You could have fooled me. Let's try again: Do you ever think about your work?

Pop: Not if I can help it.

Socrates: And when you can't help it?

Pop: I go home and hit the Jacuzzi.

Socrates: I know I shouldn't, but let me try one more time: Have you read any good books lately?

Pop: Hey, that's better, man. Nonthreatening. Soft. Mellow. Loose as a goose. Now we can interface. Soft questions are nice; hard questions are nasty.

Socrates: How about answers?

Pop: You want authors' names? Well, I'm sort of into "Beef" Skinner and Timothy Bleary.

Socrates: Do you think you can synthesize those two?

Pop: Well, if it doesn't work I can pray, "Forgive us our syntheses."

Socrates: Whom do you find useful for your work on sex?

Pop: Dr. Alex Comeforth and Dr. Brown Joy. They bring the good tidings.

Socrates: Tidings of comeforth and joy, eh?

Pop: You're catching on, man. Hey, more people read Comeforth's *Joy of Sex* than the Bible.

Socrates: I guess that's pretty obvious in practice.

Pop: And everybody knows Dr. Joy.

Socrates: I don't. I don't even know whether it's a he or a she.

Pop: You mean you know *The Joy of Sex* but not the sex of Joy?

Socrates: I guess it makes little difference.

Pop: Right you are there, man. I'm into uni.

Socrates: Uni?

Pop: Unisex. That's why I'm a feminist.

Socrates: A unisex feminist. Of course. How perfectly logical. And what is a feminist, Pop?

Pop: Women are equal to men.

Socrates: Thank you for that remarkable piece of news, but what is a feminist?

Pop: Somebody who believes the good news, man.

Socrates: I see. Well, if women are equal to men, does that mean that men are equal to women? Aren't you equally a masculinist then?

Pop: That sounds like a trick, man. No thanks to your bait. I think you're an old chauve.

Socrates: For suggesting that men are equal to women? And you are a feminist for insisting that women are equal to men? Is this a new logic, too, that you have invented?

Pop: Drop the logic, man. Stop computing. It's not in the logic. It's in the tone. The attitude. The ambiance. The milieu.

Socrates: "It"? What is this "it"?

Pop: *It,* man, *it.* Good grief, you're so out of it that you don't even know what *it* is.

Felicia: Hey, guys, this conversation is going nowhere fast. It sounds like "E.T. meets Silly Putty."

Socrates: Perhaps that's because he won't tell me what "it" is.

Felicia: Tell him, Pop.

Pop: *It* is what's happening, man.

Socrates: And what *is* happening, man?

Pop: Uni. The end of sexist stereotypes.

Socrates: What sexist stereotypes?

Pop: So-called masculine and feminine.

Socrates: So-called? I would call them archetypes, not stereotypes.

Pop: I call them old dust buckets. You probably believe in "the feminine mind" and "the masculine mind," right?

Socrates: Those terms do seem to have some meaning to me,

yes—although they are very vague.

Pop: Meaning? Dinosaur crap, man, dinosaur crap.

Socrates: So you don't think that sex is where you said fear is?

Pop: Huh? Where's that?

Socrates: Between the ears.

Pop: You mean whatever you think it is? Sure thing.

Socrates: No, not whatever you think it is. Innate and natural to the soul, the mind, the psyche as well as the soma.

Pop: Baloney. Natural, schmatural. Everything one generation thinks natural, the next finds socially relative and conditioned —including the idea of nature itself and the idea of society.

Socrates: Aha! That sounds like some philosophy at last. Tell me, then, does this socially relative conditioning include biological gender? Does the mind of society make my body male or female?

Pop: Of course not.

Socrates: So sex is innate to the body.

Pop: Hereditary rather than environmental. Yes, but not to the psyche. None of that nonsense about "the feminine mind" and "the masculine mind," please.

Socrates: Well, let's see. Here is a second question for you: What do you believe is the relation between mind and body (or perhaps we should say psyche and soma)? Do you believe, like my disciple Plato, that they are two independent substances, that we are a sort of ghost in a machine, a spirit trapped in an animal cage?

Pop: No way. Modern psychology has no patience with that Neanderthal notion. I believe in psychosomatic unity.

Socrates: And that means that the soul is not independent of the body, not insulated in its identity and its nature from the body?

Pop: Right.

Socrates: Do you see what follows from those two premises?

Pop: *Premises?*

Socrates: You speak the word as if it were in a foreign tongue. Have you ever thought those two familiar ideas together and drawn the logical conclusion from them?

Pop: Not if I could help it.

Socrates: Do you mind if I help you to do so now?

Pop: It's a free country.

Socrates: Well, see here: If biological sex is innate, and if the psychological and the biological are substantially one, not two, then psyches must be innately sexual in some way too.

Pop: Way out! Left field! You mean you think we have monosexually stamped souls?

Socrates: Stamped, yes. I'm not sure about the mono. Perhaps Jung is right about anima and animus, and we are all bisexual in our souls. But sex in the soul, yes indeed.

Pop: I suppose you think then that pure souls without bodies would be masculine or feminine too? Ghosts, or angels, or whatever?

Socrates: Good for you, Pop, a logical deduction! Yes indeed. In fact, I do not just think so; I know so. I have had some fascinating conversations with such beings, though I doubt you would believe me.

Pop: Sure you have. And how far up does this crazy sexism of yours go? What sex is God?

Socrates: God comprehends all sexes. How could he be lacking in anything?

Pop: Then why is he called "he"?

Socrates: Because to us he is masculine. To him all souls are feminine. He impregnates us, not we him. But in himself he is both.

Pop: Where the hell did you get that crazy idea?

Socrates: Not there but in heaven. But I doubt you would believe that either. You can find the idea in your Bible, though.

Pop: Where?

Socrates: Genesis 2, where it says God created us in his own image.

Pop: What's that?

Socrates: It says right there: "male and female." And since the original must have everything its image has, God must be both male and female in himself.

Pop: That's blasphemous! I'd rather be an atheist.

Socrates: But how could an atheist charge anyone with blasphemy?

Pop: Hey, I want to see how far you go with this sexism in the other direction too. If sex goes all the way up, does it go all the way down too? Are planets and water and molecules sexed too?

Socrates: Indeed they are. Have you never heard of yin and yang? Why do you suppose nearly every language has male and female nouns?

Pop: They read sex into nature, of course.

Socrates: Mightn't they read it *out of* nature?

Pop: This is crazy! Do you think sex goes all the way down into atoms?

Socrates: Surely. Positive and negative charges. More yin and yang. Feminine electrons, masculine protons. Love among the particles. Don't you see it? It's plain as the nose on your face, Pop: we're not freaks. We fit in this universe.

Pop: I think I'd *have* a fit in your freaky universe. And I suppose all those old taboos about sex fit this universe of yours too?

Socrates: Yes, but do you see why?

Pop: Because you think sex is dirty, right?

Socrates: Exactly the opposite; because it is glorious and sacred.

Pop: That doesn't make sense. If it's so good, why not liberate it, like a bird from a cage? Why hedge it in with taboos?

Socrates: Perhaps I can explain it to you by examples. Do we put taboos around paper clips?

Pop: Of course not.

Socrates: Stones?

Pop: No.

Socrates: Pennies?

Pop: No.

Socrates: What about religious objects?

Pop: Yes.

Socrates: And the names of God?

Pop: Yes.

Socrates: Do you see the general principle here?

Pop: I suppose we put taboos around what we can't explain—mysteries.

Socrates: Not quite. Is the number of stars a mystery?

Pop: Yes.

Socrates: Is the explanation of a quasar a mystery?

Pop: Yes.

Socrates: But are these things taboo?

Pop: No.

Socrates: Then it is not just mysteries that evoke taboos. Why do you think no one puts a taboo around the number of the stars?

Pop: Nobody cares.

Socrates: Exactly. But we care about sex. Or did, until the taboos were removed. You see, your demythologized era does *not* care about sex.

Pop: That's ridiculous. We're sexually free.

Socrates: You're free *from* sex. You have reduced it to merely human size—Venus is no longer a goddess—then you've reduced it to merely bodily function, then to mere social conditioning. Who could care enough about that demystified and decosmicized thing to bother with taboos?

Pop: Hmmph! So you think sex is the great cosmic mystery?

Socrates: Yes.

Pop: Or the great comic misery?

Socrates: Actually, it can be all four: cosmic, comic, mystery, or misery. Most of our jokes tell us that much.

Pop: Well, it isn't that to me.

Socrates: And of course that settles the argument.

Pop: You always love to argue, don't you? Even about sex!

Socrates: Would you rather have heat without light?

Felicia: You know, you guys, this sounds a lot like yesterday's conversation.

Pop: Felicia, you've got a very strange friend here.

Socrates: This very strange friend still does not have an answer to his last question. What would you rather have, Pop?

Pop: I'll have a corned beef on rye, I think.

Socrates: No light, then?

Pop: Light rye's O.K. To answer your question, Soc, I'll have whatever turns me on. And you don't turn me on. Your arguments give me a pain in the head. Or lower.

Socrates: Why are arguments painful to you?

Pop: They dam up my style, man.

Socrates: And your style is . . . ?

Pop: To shake loose and let it all hang out. To go with the flow. Don't argue; interface.

Socrates: We have been at cross-purposes today about something even more fundamental than sex: reason itself.

Pop: Reason's not fundamental to me.

Socrates: Obviously. You do not admit the claims of the common master, then?

Pop: No "common master" for me, man. I'm nobody's slave. I'm my own master.

Socrates: If you are your own master, then it follows that you must also be your own slave.

Pop: What? I don't dig that "it follows" routine.

Socrates: I know. That follows too.

Pop: You know, Soc, you're all tied up in that little logical straightjacket of yours.

Socrates: It's not *mine*, Pop. Reason is no one's private property. There is the argument, out there like a rock. Can you refute it?

Pop: If I want to.

Socrates: How?

Pop: Any way I want.

Socrates: There are only three ways, you know. Was there an ambiguous term, a false premise, or a logical fallacy in arguing?
Pop: Boy, do you play in a small ballpark! Narrow foul lines.
Socrates: And you refuse to play?
Pop: Oh, what the heck, why not? I'll take ambiguous terms, please. With some coffee on the side.
Socrates: Which term did we use ambiguously?
Pop: None. That's your trouble.
Socrates: Trouble?
Pop: Sure. Your terms are constipated. Loosen them up. You're walking around dressed in a suit of words ten sizes too small. It's a great relief to loosen your mind—like loosening your belt.
Socrates: And the result seems similar in both cases: something like a belch.
Pop: When you use a word, you tie it up and keep it in one place all the time, don't you?
Socrates: I try to, yes. That way I know where it is. I find it a distinct advantage to know where things are. Don't you?
Pop: Nope. Your words don't travel, man. No vacations. Dullsville.
Socrates: And you want to travel.
Pop: Right.
Socrates: But if the cities we travel to do not stay still, how can we make progress? How can you get closer to a goal that keeps receding? It's hard to hit a moving target.
Pop: You mean words are like the cities of your mind?
Socrates: *My* mind, yes. Yours looks like a cosmic earthquake.
Pop: Say, I like that: the cosmic earthquake. Is that how my mind looks?
Socrates: It's surface is riddled with fault lines.
Pop: Bad word, man. I fault the idea of fault. No-fault thinking for me.
Socrates: I don't suppose you're bothered by the fact that that idea eliminates itself?

Pop: What do you mean?

Socrates: If you fault the idea of fault, you're faulting.

Pop: But that's logic, man.

Socrates: I know. I discovered it.

Pop: Well, take it back. I don't buy it. I *like* to contradict myself. To quote my favorite poet, "Do I contradict myself? Very well, then, I contradict myself. I am large. I contain multitudes."

Socrates: But in that case, if you contradict yourself, then you do *not* contradict yourself.

Pop: Eh? What? How's that again? Run that little bugger by me once more.

Socrates: If you contradict yourself, you also admit the opposite of what you say.

Pop: Yeah. So?

Socrates: And what you say is pro-contradiction.

Pop: Yeah. Hooray for contradiction.

Socrates: And the opposite of pro-contradiction is anti-contradiction. So since you admit opposites, you admit anti-contradiction. But that's *my* logic: anti-contradiction.

Pop: Oh, that's cute, man. You juggle those little word balls like meatballs. Not me, though. Different strokes for different folks, that's my creed.

Socrates: I didn't think you had a creed.

Pop: My creed is human need. And people are different. What's O.K. for you isn't what's O.K. for me, that's my philosophy.

Socrates: I see where Felicia gets some of her... ideas, if we can call them that. This... uh... philosophy of yours, is it different from mine, then?

Pop: As different as a hot tub from an iceberg.

Socrates: And could we put the difference this way—you believe that whatever "turns you on" is good, and I do not?

Pop: That looks like a straight putt, man. Right in the hole.

Socrates: And the purpose of a definition is to limit and distinguish the idea defined from its opposites, isn't it?

Pop: If you say so, man. You're the master of definitions.

Socrates: Haven't you just defined your philosophy as refusing definitions?

Pop: Nope. You won't trap me in that one again. I don't define my philosophy at all.

Socrates: I see. And since it is definition that limits a thing, your philosophy is not limited.

Pop: Right on, man.

Socrates: So it does not exclude anything?

Pop: Right. I'm all-inclusive.

Socrates: But you do not include one thing.

Pop: What's that?

Socrates: My exclusions.

Pop: I include everything. Like God.

Socrates: Which god?

Pop: What do you mean?

Socrates: The only god I ever heard of that fits that description is Pan. His work is called pandemonium. But I don't suppose you've heard of him?

Pop: Theology's not my bag, man.

Socrates: So you also exclude theology.

Pop: I do when I feel like it, and when I don't feel like it, I don't.

Socrates: I see. You claim the privilege of contradicting yourself whenever you want.

Pop: Sure thing, man. All the time. You should try it some time. It's a real turn-on. Beats sucking lemons.

Socrates: So you claim a privilege even God does not have.

Pop: A whole slew of them, beginning with the privilege of existing.

Socrates: I see. So you *are* doing theology. But let that pass . . .

Pop: I always do.

Socrates: Yes, I see that. You know, I think I have just met a fog. There simply are no holding places in your mind.

Pop: Thanks for the compliment, man.

Socrates: I didn't mean it as a compliment. How can you compliment ooze?

Pop: That's nice: ooze. If only we ooze, we never bruise. That's why you make all those hard little distinctions: you got no ooze, man.

Socrates: You don't like my distinctions.

Pop: No way. Yuck!

Socrates: In fact, you have a *distinct* aversion to them.

Pop: Hey, I think I've had enough of this word play. I'm going home now to ooze into the Jacuzzi.

Socrates: But 'oose going into the Jacuzzi? Shouldn't a psychologist "know thyself"?

Pop: I'd rather ooze. Bye-bye, gadfly.

Socrates: Shall we meet again?

Pop: Not if I can help it.

Socrates: Perhaps you can't.

Pop: What do you mean?

Socrates: Perhaps I'm inside you as well as outside. You did use two logical thought sequences today, you know.

Pop: Hey, that's serious. Maybe I better see a shrink. Bye!

Socrates: Felicia, was that bouncing blob of ooze your guru?

Felicia: Well, I think part of me looks up to him as a guru and part of me laughs at him, like you. And the part that looks up to him is probably not the serious part. It is a lot of fun to just bounce over logic, you know.

Socrates: I know. But you have to have a logic to bounce over. It's no accident that the bounciest nonsense usually comes from logicians or mathematicians—like Lewis Carroll.

Felicia: You did some bouncing yourself. You know, I think I saw something new today. I thought you were kinda square, and Pop had all the fun. But I think you've got both halves and he's got only one. Philosophy can be fun too. Stick around some more, won't you?

Socrates: With pleasure.

11 On Communism and Capitalism

Felicia: Oh, Socrates, I'm so glad to find you here today.

Socrates: When we first met, you were not nearly so eager, remember?

Felicia: That's because I'm off drugs now and into something really meaningful. And that's what I want to talk to you about today. I want you to meet my new friend Karl. He's going to meet me here in a few minutes. He's a terribly important person to me because he's given me a great, great gift: a cause to live and work for. I was drugging because I was drifting; now I know I've got direction.

Socrates: So Karl is your new guru?

Felicia: You might say that.

Socrates: If he has truly given you a cause to live for, that is a great gift indeed, especially in this age of a plethora of means and a dearth of ends. I hope his gift is a true one and not just an apparent one.

Felicia: That's why I'm so glad you're here today, Socrates. I can't wait to hear you two in dialog. I couldn't stand up to your cross-examinations, and neither could my old guru, Pop Syke, but I'm sure Karl can. Perhaps you can even learn something from him.

Socrates: I can learn something from everyone.

Felicia: I mean he might be able to add to your wisdom.

Socrates: It is quite easy to add to zero.

Felicia: Perhaps he can even give you the gift he gave me.

Socrates: Perhaps. But I am not drifting. I have a cause to give my life for.

Felicia: Your questioning, you mean? You know, I always wanted to ask you something about that: how can it be your end and purpose in life if you never come to an end of it? Do you just seek for the sake of seeking?

Socrates: An excellent question, Felicia; in fact, the best one you have yet asked!

Felicia: And do you have an excellent answer?

Socrates: Ah, my good infection seems to be spreading, I see. Good, good! The student begins to outdo her teacher. And thus the teacher's purpose is fulfilled.

Felicia: You still haven't answered my question.

Socrates: My answer is that I seek both for the sake of seeking and for the sake of finding. If I did not seek for the sake of finding, my seeking would be dishonest. What would be the sense of looking for something if you didn't want to find it? But I also seek for the end of continued seeking. For even after I find a little of the thing I always seek—Truth—I find also this truth: that I cannot stop seeking. Philosophizing is rather like courtship in that way: even after marriage it continues, if the marriage is a good one, a living one rather than a dead one. But here! is that your new friend coming? The one with the piercing eyes and the big black mustache?

Felicia: Yes, that's Karl. Karl, Karl, over here!

Karl: Hello there, Felicia. Say, is this the Socrates fellow you spoke to me about?

Felicia: Yes. Socrates, this is my other great teacher, Karl. I hope you two can harmoniously divide my soul between you.

Socrates: Hello, Karl. What is this great gift of meaning that you seem to have given Felicia? Whatever it is, it has put a gleam in her eye and a spring in her step.

Karl: Felicia is working for the cause now.

Socrates: I hope we all work for some cause; if not, we work for nothing. But which cause? That is the question.

Karl: My cause is the people cause, the popular cause, the common cause.

Socrates: And is there a name for this common cause?

Karl: Yes. It is called Communism.

Socrates: Of course: the commonest cause. But let us not substitute a bad pun for a good definition. If you are a teacher of this cause, and I am a learner, you will answer my questions about it, won't you?

Karl: Gladly, Socrates. Will you join our cause, too, then?

Socrates: How can I know whether to join until I first know what it is? Must not knowledge precede action?

Karl: Actually, no. That's typically bourgeois logic.

Socrates: I did not know that logic itself was divided into economic classes.

Karl: Well, that is one of the new things you can learn from me. You leisured philosophers have time to speculate, but the people don't. That's your trouble: you just want to understand the world. We want to change it. You've spent thousands of years trying to understand it; it's time now for action, for real change, for the revolution. It's coming. It's happening. We're in it right now, if we'd only see it.

Adam [approaching]: Karl, are you at it again with your crazy revolutionary rabble rousing?

Karl: Adam! What are you doing here? This is no place for you. Go home and stop bothering me.

Socrates: Who is this man, Karl, and why do you refuse him the right to speak?

Karl: He's the enemy. He's a fool, Socrates.

Adam: No, *he's* the fool, Socrates. He's my kid brother. He ran away from home years ago, and he's gotten into trouble ever since.

Socrates: Is this true, Karl?

Karl: It's true that he's my brother, yes. But please don't tell the world. I'm ashamed of him.

Socrates: Fear not; the world does not hold its ear to my mouth. But why is he the enemy?

Karl: Because he's working against the cause. He's the burden I must overcome, the regressive force, the dehumanizing force, the anti-people person. He's a Capitalist!

Socrates: My, my! You spit out that word as if it were a curse. But he is your brother, is he not?

Karl: Not in spirit. The accident of having common ancestors does not make for true brotherhood.

Adam: So you are denying your roots, are you, Karl? Don't you remember Grandfather Hobbes anymore? Or Great-grandfather Machiavelli?

Socrates: Excuse me, you two, but before we get distracted into a family feud, may I continue my questions to you, Karl? I do very much want to understand why Felicia looks up to you as her teacher.

Karl: All right, Socrates. I will answer your questions for Felicia's sake and perhaps yours as well. Felicia, listen carefully.

Felicia: I always do, Karl.

Socrates: Now, Karl, did I hear you say that Adam was your brother, but not in spirit?

Karl: Yes.

Socrates: You say, then, that it is spirit that gives a man his identity?

Karl: No, no. Spirit is an illusion. All that is real is matter.

Socrates: What about mind?

Karl: Never mind.

Socrates: Again we substitute a bad pun for a good definition.

Karl: Mind is an epiphenomenon: an effect but not a cause. The brain produces thought as the liver produces bile. Thought is like the heat generated by electricity: it doesn't do the work, it's just a by-product. Like the puff of smoke that comes out of the exhaust pipe of a car.

Socrates: I see. Like a fart.

Karl: There is no need to be rude.

Socrates: But there is a need to understand. Are you not saying that thought is like a fart? May I not accurately label your epiphenomenalism the Fart Theory of Thought?

Karl: Sticks and stones may break my bones, but names will never hurt me.

Socrates: I did not mean to hurt, only to accurately label.

Karl: Well, you haven't accurately labeled my cause yet. Don't you want to hear about that?

Socrates: I certainly do. And I would also like to hear from your brother Adam, who has been listening so patiently to us.

Karl: No you wouldn't. He is the enemy of the people, I tell you.

Socrates: That was the label they put on me when they executed me. I have a certain sympathy for victims of false labeling. So I would like to hear both of you, and then decide whether you, or he, or both, are guilty of false labeling.

Karl: You're wasting your time, Socrates. You keep wanting to understand things and you never get around to changing them. Join my cause now and I'll show you the real march of the people into the promised land . . .

Adam: See, Socrates? He's always been like that: one-sided. He won't let me speak. But I'll let him speak. It is I who champion freedom. The free market of ideas—that's my way.

Karl: Don't let him deceive you, Socrates. Only under Communism is there true freedom.

Adam: That's absurd, Karl. Why then do your people persecute dissenters? How can you say there is freedom under totalitarian control?

Karl: It is the people who control. And the control must be total to guarantee freedom: freedom from poverty, from ignorance, from unemployment, from foreign domination . . .

Adam: Is that all you mean by freedom? What about freedom of thought?

Karl: Thought is a mere epiphenomenon. The real freedom is in the real realm, the realm of matter.

Adam: See, Socrates? You and I, we are the spiritual brothers. You're on my side, not his.

Socrates: But the freedom *you* speak of, Adam, is it not the free market?

Adam: Yes. He wants the state to own everything. I'm for freedom of the private sector. "That government is best which governs least."

Socrates: But do you not see that your definition of freedom is just as materialistic and economistic as his?

Adam: Oh, well, I'm also for freedom of thought and speech.

Socrates: You seem to bring that in as an afterthought. As if a free-market economy were the primary thing. Isn't it true that freedom of thought is not confined to Capitalism, not the specific defining factor of Capitalism, but a free-market economy is?

Adam: Yes.

Socrates: Then you could have Capitalism without freedom of thought, and you could have freedom of thought without Capitalism, in principle.

Adam: But in fact, Capitalism has always gone together with freedom of thought, and Communism has always opposed it.

Socrates: I wish to argue about principles rather than historical facts. Your brother discouraged me from that. Do you discourage me too?

Adam: No. I'm all for the principle of free thought and free speech. That's why you should be on my side. You got executed for defending free speech, didn't you?

Socrates: Why do you think that?

Adam: I've read your masterpiece of a speech at your trial many times. It's one of my great inspirations.

Socrates: The *Apology*, you mean? You must have misread it many times, then. I never spoke of freedom of speech.

Adam: Wasn't that what you got executed for?

Socrates: No. I was executed for corrupting the youth of the state and for not believing in the gods of the state.

Adam: But you yourself point out in that speech that the real charge against you was that you were a philosopher.

Socrates: That is correct.

Adam: And a philosopher is a free thinker.

Socrates: A philosopher is a lover of wisdom. Does a lover desire above all freedom? Does not a lover desire above all to be bound forever to his beloved?

Adam: Do you agree with Karl, then, that the right of free thought and free speech is not important?

Socrates: No.

Adam: Then why did you not invoke those rights in your *Apology*?

Socrates: Because they were not my defense. My life was not devoted to them as my primary good.

Adam: What was it devoted to, then?

Socrates: Wisdom and virtue. The true and the good.

Adam: But isn't freedom of thought and speech a necessary means to those things?

Socrates: Perhaps, though I do not see how freedom of *speech* can be necessary for them.

Adam: Why not?

Socrates: If one thing is necessary for another, then when you take the first thing away, you cannot have the second, isn't that so?

Adam: Yes.

Socrates: Well, then, do you think that when you take away a person's right to free speech, you remove wisdom and virtue from him? When you bind and gag a prisoner, do you make him foolish and vicious?

Adam: No.

Socrates: Then free speech is not necessary for wisdom and virtue.

Adam: Are you opposing free speech now, like Karl?

Socrates: Certainly not. I say only what I say: that it is not necessary for wisdom and virtue.

Adam: Freedom is not important, then?

Socrates: I did not say that either.

Adam: But it is not important for the highest things, wisdom and virtue?

Socrates: I do not say that either. There is another kind of freedom which seems to be absolutely necessary for wisdom and virtue, and that is simply free will, the freedom we all have by virtue of our very nature. This was not given to us by the state and cannot be removed by the state, even a totalitarian state, and therefore it need not be defended against the state—that would seem to follow, wouldn't it?

Adam: No! We must defend our liberties!

Karl: See, Adam? Socrates is on my side more than yours. Remember, it was his student Plato who first invented Communism, in the *Republic.*

Socrates: I'm afraid that's another misreading of the texts. Plato did write about a kind of Communism, if all you mean by that is the abolition of private property. But it was only to be for the small ruling class, not all the people. But here, Adam, I am not finished with you. I have still to learn what your ends are.

You have learned mine—wisdom and virtue—but I have not learned yours, even though I am supposed to be questioning you and learning from you rather than you from me. The system you prefer must be preferred for a reason. What is the reason? For what is Capitalism better? For what end is it a better means?

Adam: Prosperity, Socrates. Capitalist nations have a much higher standard of living than Communist nations. Our system works, theirs doesn't. History has tested and proved us to be right.

Socrates: I see. Capitalism is a more efficient means to prosperity. And what is prosperity for? Is it the end, or is it a means to any further end?

Adam: It is for whatever you want it to be for. You make your fortune and then you are free to spend it as you like. You see, we have freedom and they don't.

Socrates: So your system of Capitalism does not give you the end, but only the means.

Adam: Yes. You are free to choose your own end. The state does not dictate it to you.

Socrates: But if you do not know the true end of human life, how can you know that the Capitalist means is a good means?

Adam: I don't understand.

Socrates: A means is a good one if and only if it attains the end for which it is a means, isn't that right?

Adam: Yes.

Socrates: A shovel is a good means for digging, and a poor means for eating; a fork is a good means for eating but a poor means for digging.

Adam: Right. Means are relative.

Socrates: Relative to ends, yes. Well, then, just suppose that the ends I devoted my life to—wisdom and virtue—are in fact the true ends. I have not proved to you that they are, but you have not proved that they are not, either. So they *may* be. Well, if wisdom and virtue are the true ends of human life, and if prosperity is not a good means to wisdom and virtue—if rich people are not necessarily better or wiser than poor people—then prosperity is not such a good thing after all. Does that not follow?

Adam: But of course prosperity is good. Everyone wants it. Everyone is agreed about that.

Socrates: Except your wise men. And should we measure goods by the standards of the wise or by the standards of the foolish?

Adam: The wise. But . . .

Socrates: Well? Do not all the wise warn of the temptations of riches? Isn't it true that Jesus spoke of almost nothing more frequently than this?

Adam: But Socrates, what do you say the end of the state is, if not prosperity and the liberty to get it?

Socrates: Virtue.

Adam: That's foolish, Socrates. Virtue cannot be the business of the state. The state cannot make people virtuous. That's the error of Karl and his cause. People make the state, not vice versa. In my system, the state does not hinder the individual from pursuing virtue. But it does not try to impose virtue upon him.

Socrates: But do you think a state has nothing to do with virtue? Can't the state at least make it easier for people to be virtuous? Wouldn't this be a good definition of the good state, in fact— "that state which makes it easier to be virtuous is a good state." That would seem to be what is left if we reject the idea that the state is what *makes* us virtuous *and* the idea that the state has nothing to do with virtue at all. A kind of reasonable middle position.

Adam: Why do you reject the idea that the state has no business at all trying to make us virtuous?

Socrates: Do you want to separate means and ends, state and virtue, completely?

Adam: I want the state to leave people free.

Socrates: And not to help people toward virtue?

Adam: Not to push.

Socrates: Is all helping pushing?

Adam: No. But I want to maintain freedom.

Socrates: Does all helping toward virtue remove freedom?

Adam: Depends on what kind of help, I guess.

Socrates: Let us consider an example. Does a good parent help his child toward virtue?

Adam: Yes.

Socrates: And does a good parent respect the child's freedom?

Adam: Yes.

Socrates: And is help toward virtue a threat to the child's freedom?

Adam: Not necessarily.

Socrates: Then why can't the state do the same to its citizens?

Adam: Because the citizens are adults, not children. You want to make the state paternalistic.

Socrates: Or maternalistic. Yes, I do. You see, I do not think we *are* adults spiritually—ever. Do you think you have stopped growing in virtue?

Adam: No, but it is not the state that is our moral tutor.

Socrates: The business of the state is business, then?

Adam: Yes.

Socrates: And in your system, prosperity comes from capital?

Adam: Yes.

Socrates: And capital is profit?

Adam: Yes.

Socrates: And profit is not automatic, but comes about only with intelligent effort?

Adam: Yes.

Socrates: So your system is based on the profit motive.

Adam: Yes.

Socrates: Do you know what moralists call the profit motive?

Adam: What?

Socrates: Greed.

Adam: A person's motives are not the business of the state,

Socrates

Socrates: Oh, but it is. Without this motive—declared vicious and immoral by almost all the great moralists—your system will not work. What do you think would happen to a Capitalist nation if everyone practiced the greedlessness of Jesus, or Buddha, or even Thoreau?

Adam: The economy would collapse.

Socrates: Exactly. So the state *is* founded on something in the realm of morality. But it is not a virtue; it is a vice.

Karl: Congratulations, Socrates. You've demolished the folly of my evil brother almost as well as I could. Now you see that you must join my cause. Capitalism is based on greed. So join me in removing the temptation to greed. Remove private property and you remove the possibility of greed.

Socrates: Alas, you do not. Why can't I be as greedy for property owned by the state as for property owned by my neighbor?

Karl: The state is the people. The state *is* my neighbor.

Socrates: Then I can be greedy for more of what my neighbor has.

Karl: But at least my state makes it easier for people to be virtuous, as you say. The temptation to greed is much less, because there's no hope of amassing a private hoard. People are much more greedy for what they hope to gain than for what there is no hope of gaining.

Socrates: Is that why you want to eliminate private property? Because it tempts us to immoral greed?

Karl: Actually, no. That is not my motive, but yours. But we can work for the same end, even if we have different reasons for it.

Socrates: What are your reasons, if they are not the same as mine, for wanting to abolish capital and private profit? And why do you not share my reason?

Karl: I'm not a moralist, like you. Remember, I'm a materialist, a realist.

Socrates: I see. What are your reasons, then?

Karl: For abolishing capital?

Socrates: Yes.

Karl: It is the instrument by which the rich oppress the poor. By it, the rich get richer and the poor get poorer. Those who do not have it must sell themselves and their labor. Capitalism alienates and dehumanizes the masses.

Socrates: That sounds pretty moralistic to me. But rather than going into a long exploration of the meanings of those long terms of yours, let me just ask you one simple little question. What is the *end* of your system?

Karl: We overcome alienation and class distinction, and harness all to the common task.

Socrates: The common task—what is that?

Karl: Of the state, you mean?

Socrates: Yes.

Karl: Production, of course. We remove the means of production from the oppressors and return it to the people.

Socrates: I am not asking *who* but *why*. Production is your end? Production of what?

Karl: Everything people need.

Socrates: Things.

Karl: Yes. But things are for people.

Socrates: For people to have?

Karl: For people to use. Adam's end is having; mine is using. His is the private good, mine is the common good.

Socrates: Whether it is having or using, it is *things* you are both talking about, then.

Karl: Of course.

Socrates: And many things constitutes prosperity.

Karl: Yes.

Socrates: Then your end is the same as your brother's: material prosperity. It is only your means that is different.

Karl: That cannot be!

Socrates: What, then, is the difference in ends between you?

Karl: He is working for the few, I for the many.

Adam: That's a lie, Socrates. My system is for the many too. Capitalism makes *everyone* richer. And history has proved that.

Karl: You fool! The past belongs to you, but the future belongs to us. We will triumph!

Socrates: But Karl, even if you are right and you are the champion of the many while Adam is the champion of the few, even if you work for the poor while Adam works for the rich, still, it is the same goal that you both seek: you for the many and he for the few *or* for the many: riches. And there's nothing new in that. It is a very old answer to the great question of the *summum bonum*, the greatest good. Your two systems are only two new social means to the same old end. If the end is not a good one, what great difference does it make which means is more effective in leading to it?

Karl and Adam [together]: This cannot be!

Socrates: What do you think about all this, Felicia?

Felicia: Socrates, I think you've done it again! You've de-gurued my guru. He's no better than his brother. Karl, I'm sorry but I must think about all this a lot more before I can join your cause.

Karl: Felicia, this babbler has seduced you with a decadent bourgeois tool, abstract speculation. You have thrown away action in exchange for mere thought. It is we who will change the world, you know, while you join this mere thinker in merely thinking about it.

Felicia: I think I have to get my own life in order first before I change the world, Karl. If I don't know what's really good, how can I help others to find it?

Karl: That is another seduction, Felicia: individualism. Don't you realize that all your thoughts are social products? They have no independent validity.

Felicia: In that case, Karl, the same holds for you and your thoughts. The thought that thought is a mere social product is also a mere social product, and the thought that thought has no independent validity also has no independent validity. Your theory refutes itself. Why should I listen to you? If you're right, you can't help how your tongue happens to wag. You're nothing but a product of the social forces determining you, just as much as Socrates is.

Karl: Alas, Felicia, you have become a decadent bourgeois logician.

Felicia: Alas, Karl, you have become a name-caller instead of a wise man.

Socrates: And *you* have become a first-rate philosopher, Felicia! I couldn't have done better myself with that last exchange.

Felicia: Thanks—I think. It just cost me a friend. There he goes, off in a huff, with his brother.

Socrates: Truth is always a better friend than any who cannot endure its company.

Interlude before Felicia's Oxford Tutorial

Felicia: Socrates, I don't know whether to thank you or resent you. You've taken away the only five things that ever really turned me on.

Socrates: You mean pot, rock, free sex, and your two gurus?

Felicia: Yes. I feel robbed.

Socrates: I hope I am only a grave robber.

Felicia: What do you mean by that?

Socrates: I try to rob you only of dead ideas, not live ones.

Felicia: At least my last guru, Karl, gave me a cause to work for. I'm not sure it's better to work for no cause than for a bad one.

Socrates: Is it better to eat poison or not to eat?

Felicia: Isn't it better to eat bad food than no food at all, and starve?

Socrates: Not if there is good food to be had. Refusing bad food is the way to keep your stomach available for good food, is it not?

Felicia: I guess so. *If* there's good food to be had.

Socrates: So you doubt that?

Felicia: Yes. You've made me doubt everything. It's not a comfortable feeling. I'm not sure you've done more good than harm.

Socrates: Ah, but you can use even the apparent harm, the uncomfortable feeling, for good. Doubt can be a way to find truth, the soul's food. You see, Felicia, I gave you the best thing I could. I could not give you the greatest thing in the world, Truth, because no man can give that; it does not come from us. So I gave you the next best thing, the way to it. I think a doubt, a question, is the second most valuable thing in the world, just as the road home is the second most valuable thing, next to home itself, because it is the way to it.

Felicia: I think I see. The means to the greatest end is the second greatest thing.

Socrates: You do see. You know, you are a natural philosopher. Once you freed yourself from your addictions, your mind grew like a plant.

Felicia: It's still only a seedling.

Socrates: That realization is the surest proof that it is alive and growing.

Felicia: But I have one more big question for you, Socrates, and it's much bigger than any we've talked about yet. Perhaps we should set aside tomorrow to talk about it.

Socrates: I would be pleased to do that. What is the question?

Felicia: Well, we just agreed that questions are the second greatest things only because they lead to Truth, the first thing. But suppose that first thing is unattainable? Suppose there are no real answers, only more questions?

Socrates: Ah, you want to talk about the issue of skepticism.

Felicia: Yes, but not skepticism of everything. That's silly. Of course we know that two and two are four, and that the sun shines. But questions about values, questions about good and evil, questions about the meaning of life—all the really important questions. There doesn't seem to be any hard and fast answer to them, no answer that's true for everyone. I can't help wondering whether all the really important things aren't just matters of opinion, whether values aren't just subjective.

Socrates: The question you have asked is a great one indeed, Felicia, and a far more important one than any we have yet dealt with. In fact, I think this question is the most important question for your entire civilization. For it is about the idea that every previous society believed in and which yours does not, the idea that values are objective. This difference is surely far more important than any other difference between civilizations. Yours will be known to future ages not first of all as the society which put a man on the moon, or which invented atomic weapons, but the society which denied objective values.

Felicia: I know that's a very important difference, but why is it more important than any other? Past societies differed a lot about values too. They often fought wars about those differences.

Socrates: Yes, but even if one society worships Jehovah and another worships Allah, even if one worships cats and another worships the sun, even if one worships peace and another worships war, all at least worship something. Yours is the first that does not.

Felicia: Many people still do.

Socrates: As individuals, yes. But not as a society.

Felicia: I see. It may be the crucial question for my society, but I'm asking it because it's also the crucial question for me. You see, you've started me on a road, Socrates—the road of philosophizing—and I have to know that that road leads somewhere before I walk far down it. And I'm especially interested in this question right now because I had a talk with Peter Pragma this morning, and he told me about the conversations he had with you, especially the last one, the one about the meaning of life, or the greatest good. I thought your arguments were great,

Socrates, except for one crucial missing link. Throughout that conversation you both were assuming without question that there *was* one right and true answer to the question of the highest value. You assumed that the good is objective, that values aren't just relative to the individual's opinion. But you didn't prove that. Almost all of my teachers and textbooks don't seem to believe that, and I don't know whether I do either.

Socrates: For a question of such primary importance to you as well as your society I am very glad we decided to set aside a longer time tomorrow. I think we should also decide on some rules of procedure, a "game plan," so to speak, so that we do not wander about in this often confusing wilderness.

Felicia: What exactly do you mean by a game plan?

Socrates: I think we should determine in advance who must prove what, so that you can prepare.

Felicia: Who must prove what?

Socrates: Yes. Is the onus of proof on the objectivist or the subjectivist? On me to prove values are objective or on you to prove that they are subjective?

Felicia: On you, I hope. You're not trying to get the easier task before we start, are you?

Socrates: No, I am trying to decide how best we can find the truth together, not who will win, as if we were opponents rather than allies.

Felicia: Fine. But what difference does this "onus of proof" make? I'm still not clear what you mean.

Socrates: If the onus of proof is on me, on objectivism, then our procedure will be to assume your position, subjectivism, at the start . . .

Felicia: That sounds good to me.

Socrates: And then any one good argument by me against it suffices to demolish and refute it.

Felicia: Oh. You mean I have to answer all your objections?

Socrates: Yes, to be sure that the one fatal, unanswerable objection does not emerge to destroy you.

Felicia: What about the other way 'round?

Socrates: Then, if the onus of proof is on you, all you must do is to find *one* fatal objection to my objectivism, but what I must do is answer *every* one of your objections. If I fail even once, you win.

Felicia: Well, then, Socrates, I accept the onus of proof. I shall attack your objectivism, and you must defend it. That will even the odds between us a bit.

Socrates: Why do you think so?

Felicia: Because it's always easier to attack than to defend.

Socrates: Is it? I wonder. But there is another reason why I think this is best. I should defend objectivism and you should attack it because that is how our history went. We began with objectivism. It is thousands of years old. Subjectivism is the rebel, the upstart. And the onus of proof is always on the rebel.

Felicia: I agree. Let's retrace our history.

Socrates: There is one other suggestion I should like to make, but it is only appropriate for a teacher.

Felicia: Make it. You're my teacher. The teacher without a classroom.

Socrates: The world is my classroom. All right, here is my suggested teaching method. Did you ever hear of the Oxford tutorial system?

Felicia: Yes. The student writes a paper defending a position and reads it to a teacher in private, and the teacher tears it apart.

Socrates: Evaluates it, comments on it, dissects it, dialogs with the student about it.

Felicia: Sort of your Socratic method but starting with writing rather than speaking, right?

Socrates: Yes. So I suggest we try it tomorrow. I think it would help to sort out the arguments about such a complex and important issue. Why don't you go write a little essay attacking objectivism and read it to me, and then I shall question you about what you wrote.

Felicia: O.K. Can I get my professors and friends and textbooks to help me?

Socrates: Why not? You want the strongest arguments you can get, don't you?

Felicia: It's a deal, then, Socrates. An Oxford tutorial tomorrow with the inventor of the Socratic method: I can hardly wait.

12 On Objective Values

Socrates: Well, Felicia, here we are again in our outdoor classroom in the groves of academe. Are you ready for your Oxford tutorial?

Felicia: Yes, Socrates. You know, I'm still not sure who you are or how you got here, but I'm grateful for your free teaching.

Socrates: How could I put a price on the priceless?

Felicia: Desperate State University does. The tuition rises each year.

Socrates: Indeed. How could my pupil Plato ever have foreseen that his great invention of the university would one day be in such a desperate state? Or that it would take twenty-four centuries for bread to become smorgasbord? But here—are you ready to read to me your paper, as we planned, defending the subjectivity of values?

Felicia: Yes, Socrates, and I'm glad it's a warm and sunny morning, because I think this is going to take some time. My paper is quite short, but your method of cross-examination is usually very long.

Socrates: That's because I think many errors take place through haste, and perhaps this is especially true about errors concerning values.

Felicia: You know, maybe we can save ourselves a lot of sweat. Maybe neither of us is in error. Maybe values are whatever we think they are, so that if I think they're subjective, why then they're subjective to me, and if you think they're objective, well, then, they're objective—to you.

Socrates: That is a statement of your position but not of mine. I do not believe values are objective *to me*; I believe they are objective. "Objective to me"—what possible sense could that make? Is that not the same sort of contradiction as "subjective in themselves"?

Felicia: You mean "objective to me" equals "objective subjectively" and "subjective in themselves" equals "subjective objectively"?

Socrates: Something like that. I think we had better define our terms before we begin. For if we cannot meaningfully agree about the meaning of the terms *values, subjective* and *objective,* then we cannot meaningfully disagree about whether values are objective or subjective.

Felicia: That was going to be the first point in my paper: defining my terms.

Socrates: Excellent, Felicia. Excuse me for anticipating you. What are your definitions?

Felicia: They're very simple. I mean by *values* simply "rightness and wrongness," by *objective* simply "independent of the human mind" and by *subjective* "dependent on the human mind." How's that?

Socrates: I think those are fine definitions: they are simple and clear, and they are what people usually mean by those words.

Now let us get to your arguments against the objectivity of values.

Felicia: I found seven arguments, Socrates. Here they are.

The first argument is unanswerable because it is based on undeniable facts: the facts discovered by sociologists and anthropologists. The fact is simply that individuals and cultures *do* have very different values, different moralities. As Descartes says, you can't imagine any idea so strange that it hasn't been taught by some philosopher. And you can't imagine any morality so weird that it hasn't been taught by some society. Anyone who thinks values aren't relative to culture simply doesn't know much about other cultures.

Here's a second argument, also based on a fact. The fact is that we are conditioned by our society, differently conditioned by different societies. If I had been born in a Hindu society, I would have Hindu values today. We don't discover values as we discover planets; we *have* them as we have measles: we catch them from our society.

My third argument is practical, from the *consequences* of believing subjectivism or objectivism. The consequence of subjectivism is tolerance; the consequence of objectivism is intolerance and dogmatism and trying to impose your values on others because you think everyone ought to believe your way. If you believe values are only *yours,* you don't try to force people to believe in them, unless you want to force them to believe in *you.*

My fourth argument is the primacy of motive. To do the right thing for the wrong reason is wrong, but you can't blame someone for doing the wrong thing for the right reason, the right motive. Morality is a matter of the heart, motive, and that's obviously subjective.

My fifth argument is circumstances, or the situation. Moral choices are conditioned by the situation, and that's relative to thousands of things. There can't be the same rules for all situations. You can imagine an exception to every rule in some situation. For instance, it can be good to kill if you kill a homicidal aggressor, good to steal if you steal a weapon from a madman, good to lie if you're the Dutch lying to the Nazis about where the Jews are hiding. There's no absolute morality; it's always relative to the situation.

My sixth argument is that it makes no sense to call an objective act good or evil. When you see an evil deed, like a murder, you feel terrible; the morality is in our feelings, in how we feel about the act, not in the act itself. Where's the evil? In the gun? The arm? The trigger finger? The wound? Those are simply facts. We interpret the facts in terms of our feelings. We add value colors to the black-and-white world of physical facts.

My seventh argument is that objective values would mean we are not free. Either we are free to create our own values, or values are imposed on us as a hammer is imposed on a nail. To preserve human dignity we must preserve human freedom, and to preserve human freedom we must preserve our creativity, our ability to create our own values freely.

Well, there you are, Socrates. It was short, as I said, and I hope sweet too.

Socrates: There is no question about its being short, but I have a few questions about its sweetness.

Felicia: Somehow I thought you would.

Socrates: My first question is about your term "values."

Felicia: I thought you agreed with my definition of it.

Socrates: I do. But I wonder whether you mean by it the *law* of right and wrong, or just the *feeling* of right and wrong.

Felicia: The feeling of right and wrong.

Socrates: So you would rather talk about moral values than about moral law.

Felicia: Yes.

Socrates: That's what I was afraid of. I fear you beg the question in your terminology. As you use it, the very word "values" connotes something subjective rather than something objective:

feelings rather than laws. So for you to speak of "objective values" would be as self-contradictory as for me to speak of "subjective laws." I think your reluctance to talk about moral laws really means you believe there *are* no moral laws.

Felicia: Of course there are moral laws. The Ten Commandments, for instance. But that's old familiar stuff. Everybody knows that.

Socrates: Could you recite the Ten Commandments, since they are so familiar?

Felicia: Well... thou shalt not steal, thou shalt not kill, thou shalt not commit adultery....

Socrates: Yes?

Felicia: That's all I remember right now...

Socrates: Three out of ten. Perhaps it is an illusion that everyone knows that old familiar stuff. Or perhaps you are the only one who forgot the other seven?

Felicia: All right, so I'm not an expert in the moral laws. We're talking about moral *values* today, aren't we?

Socrates: About whether they are laws or feelings. If they are laws, then you are not an expert in moral values, since you are not an expert in moral laws.

Felicia: So I'm not an expert. Lesson One again. You've made your point.

Socrates: Perhaps not sufficiently, if you are so impatient to move beyond it so quickly.

Felicia: You really love to get in your favorite point, don't you?

Socrates: It is not my favorite point by any means; it is quite embarrassing, in fact. But it must be truly believed and fully realized; that is the one thing I know. The point with regard to knowledge is that there are only two kinds of people in the world: the foolish, who think they are wise, and the wise, who know they are foolish. The same point with regard to morality is that there are only two kinds of people: sinners, who think they are saints, and saints, who know they are sinners. I will never cease to teach this embarrassing truth because without it, I am convinced, there simply *is* no knowledge and no morality, only the deceptive appearances of them.

Felicia: Humility first, eh?

Socrates: Exactly. Do you know what St. Bernard answered when someone asked him what were the first four virtues?

Felicia: What?

Socrates: Humility, humility, humility and humility.

Felicia: He wasn't impatient to go beyond that, is that it?

Socrates: Yes. And now you?

Felicia: All right, Socrates. I'm a fool too.

Socrates: Good. Then we belong together, we two. Now let us get back to your paper, since we know who we are.

Felicia: All right. Remember, if you can't refute every one of my objections to objective values, I will have proved my thesis.

Socrates: Agreed. Now then, your first argument was that scientists have discovered that different cultures have different moralities, isn't that correct?

Felicia: Yes.

Socrates: And you claimed this argument was unanswerable because it was based on a fact, isn't that right?

Felicia: Yes.

Socrates: So you presuppose that all arguments that are based on facts are unanswerable?

Felicia: Yes.

Socrates: But surely that is a mistake in logic?

Felicia: What do you mean?

Socrates: Can't you make a logically unwarranted inference from a fact?

Felicia: Oh. Of course. But how do you think I did that?

Socrates: By using your ambiguous term "values." Value-opinions or value-feelings are one thing; true, real, objective values would be another thing, wouldn't they?

Felicia: Yes, if they existed. But now you're begging the question in assuming that they exist.

Socrates: I am assuming nothing, merely clarifying two different meanings of a term.

Felicia: So what's your point?

Socrates: Though value-opinions may be relative to different cultures and subjective to individuals, that does not necessarily mean that real values are. For even if people's opinions about anything vary with time or place or weather or digestion or the prejudices of teachers, that does not prove that the thing itself varies in these ways, does it?

Felicia: But *this* thing is values, "right and wrong." But right and wrong *are* matters of opinion, or conviction. So when opinions or convictions vary, right and wrong vary.

Socrates: Ah, but that is precisely the question at issue: *are* right and wrong just matters of opinion? You are begging the question, assuming exactly the conclusion you must prove: that right and wrong are matters of subjective opinion.

Felicia: Oh.

Socrates: Not only that, there is a second and even simpler mistake in your argument: it is *not* based on a fact.

Felicia: What? Of course it is. Don't you know about different cultures?

Socrates: Of course; I am from one myself. But scientists have not proved that values are relative or subjective for the simple reason that they have never observed values. Values cannot be measured by scientific instruments.

Felicia: Value-opinions, then. They have gone to many different places and taken opinion polls, you know.

Socrates: I know. And even there you are simply mistaken about the facts. Even value-opinions are not wholly relative to cultures or individuals.

Felicia: What? Of course they are. Don't you know your social sciences? You're simply ignoring the facts.

Socrates: Let us see who is ignoring the facts. Let's look closely at some of the facts you appeal to to prove your point. Could you give a few examples?

Felicia: Certainly. Suicide, for instance, is honorable for an ancient Roman or in Japan, but not for a Jew or a Christian. Usury was wrong in the Middle Ages but right today. It's wrong to bare your breasts in England, but not in the South Seas. Value-opinions vary tremendously. That's a fact.

Socrates: But not totally. And that is another fact. Doesn't every society have some code of honor, and justice, and modesty (to speak only of your three examples)?

Felicia: I think so . . .

Socrates: So those three value-opinions, at any rate, are universal. No society prizes dishonor above honor, or injustice above justice, or immodesty above modesty. And there are many more things like this. Perhaps we should call these things "principles"—I mean things like the law of fair play and courage and generosity and honesty and unselfishness. I know that the rules of behavior differ greatly, but different rules of behavior seem designed to differently apply or obey the same principles. For instance, both South Sea Island dress and English dress are for modesty as well as for beauty and perhaps for other things as well. No society feels the same way about the sexual organs as it feels about the other parts of the body, does it?

Felicia: I think not. So you're distinguishing the principles from the rules, and saying the values are in the principles rather than the rules, and that the principles are the same for everyone?

Socrates: Yes—even that *opinions* about principles are the same for everyone, or nearly everyone. Did you ever hear of anyone who valued dishonesty above honesty? Or a society that rewarded homicidal maniacs and punished life-saving surgeons?

Felicia: No. So what is the relation between principles and rules?

Socrates: I think it is rather like the relation between meaning and expression. The same meaning can be expressed differently,

or in different languages. So the same value can be expressed in
different codes of rules. If there were no common meaning, it
would be impossible to translate from one language to another.
And if there were no common principles, we could not even
argue about which set of rules was better, because we would
have no common meaning to "better."

Felicia: You mean we couldn't even be doing what we're doing
now, arguing about morality?

Socrates: Right. Now here's a fact: people do argue about morality. They nearly always assume the same principles, and each
tries to prove he or she is right according to those principles.
No one argues about whether it's better to be fair or unfair, loyal
or disloyal, full of hate or full of love. They argue not about principles but applications.

Felicia: I see. That sounds like a very simple point, the distinction between principles and applications. How could so many of
our leading thinkers have missed it?

Socrates: Perhaps because they were not "leading thinkers" at
all, but following thinkers, sheep with their nose to the tail of
the Zeitgeist.

Felicia: But don't you think older societies often absolutized
their relativities and exalted their applications into principles?
They had their nose to the tail of their Zeitgeist too.

Socrates: Yes, and your society relativizes absolutes, and de-
motes principles to the level of applications. Two wrongs don't
make a right, and two mistakes don't make a truth. They are
simply opposite errors.

Felicia: But Socrates, just because most societies so far have
agreed about many values, that doesn't mean there can't be a
society that comes up with a new value tomorrow.

Socrates: No society has ever invented a new value, Felicia.
That would be like inventing a new sound, or a new color. All we
can do is put the primary sounds or colors together in new ways.

Felicia: Then what happened in Nazi Germany? Didn't they

create new values?

Socrates: Certainly not. They just denied old ones. The only radical novelty in values that any society has ever come up with has been negations. Just as an occasional individual shows up who is color blind, or tone deaf. But no one ever shows up who sees a color no one ever saw before, or hears a note no one ever heard before.

Felicia: I wonder. Isn't an individual free to go by any rules at all?

Socrates: Do you think you are?

Felicia: Perhaps.

Socrates: I think not, and I think I can show you that.

Felicia: Go ahead.

Socrates: Do you think I am also free to create wholly new values and live by them?

Felicia: If I am, you are too.

Socrates: Very well, then, let us experiment and test your theory.

Felicia: How?

Socrates: By my announcing my new value system. It is this: I have won the argument with you simply because I am much older than you are. I also have sharper eyesight. I do not need glasses, as you do. Therefore I am wiser than you.

Felicia: That's silly, Socrates. You can't win an argument just because you're older and don't wear glasses.

Socrates: Those are my values. If I were teaching a class and you were in it, you would pass my course only if you were one of the older students and needed no glasses.

Felicia: That's not fair.

Socrates: But what is "fair"? Fairness, or justice, is merely subjective and relative, remember? It is whatever I make it. How dare you now assume some objective and universal standard of justice to which you expect me to conform? Why should I conform to your subjective standard of justice? What right do you have to impose your personal, subjective values on me? My subjective standard is just as valid as yours if there is no objective standard. And I say justice is age and sight. But to my arbitrary subjectivism you now reply with the old idea of a single objective justice or "fairness" that you expect me to know and obey. So the cat is out of the bag; you are an objectivist after all, in practice. Your subjectivism in theory was only a disguise.

Felicia: All right, Socrates, you win round one. Let's go to round two, all right? How do you demolish my second objection?

Socrates: Would you summarize it for me first, please?

Felicia: Yes. Society conditions values in us. If I had been born into a Hindu society I would have Hindu values.

Socrates: Once again that slippery word "values." We must bear in mind the distinction we agreed to. What society conditions in us, what we *have*, is *opinions* about values. But to identify these with values themselves is to beg the question once again, is it not?

Felicia: But at least society determines those value opinions.

Socrates: Determines or conditions?

Felicia: What's the difference?

Socrates: An artist's palette and brushes condition his painting, but they leave him free to choose within the bounds set by his conditioning. Parents condition their children not to steal, but the children are free to disobey. Conditioning leaves you free. Determining does not.

Felicia: My sociology textbooks don't make that distinction.

Socrates: That's because their writers are not philosophers.

Felicia: I still think if I were born a Hindu I'd have Hindu values.

Socrates: Has everyone who was born into a Hindu society grown up to accept Hindu values? Or are there rebels, nonconformists? Do some Hindus become Christians, or Marxists?

Felicia: Yes.

Socrates: Then they are only conditioned, not determined.

Felicia: All right, but they do condition us, at least. We do learn different values from different societies.

Socrates: Not wholly different values, as we have already seen. No society teaches us cowardice, or selfishness.

Felicia: Partially different values, then. But that, at least is a fact.

Socrates: Let us look more closely at this fact. You speak of "society" as an agent. "Society" means teachers, does it not? Especially parents?

Felicia: Yes. Why do you have to say that?

Socrates: Because "society" sounds so abstract and ghostly, like the thing I could not defend myself against in my *Apology:* the Zeitgeist, or public opinion, or "what everyone knows." It is always helpful to be concrete. So let us substitute "teachers" for "society" in our argument. All right?

Felicia: All right.

Socrates: Would you say this is your argument then—that values are subjective because we learn them from our society, that is, our teachers?

Felicia: Yes.

Socrates: Do you see the hidden premise?

Felicia: Let's see . . . that what we learn from society is subjective?

Socrates: What we learn from *teachers* is subjective. Yes. Now is this true? Is everything we learn from teachers subjective?

Felicia: I don't know.

Socrates: Did you learn the laws of physics from teachers?

Felicia: Yes.

Socrates: Are they subjective?

Felicia: No.

Socrates: Then not everything we learn from teachers is subjective.

Felicia: But teachers disagree. We learn different things from different teachers. They can't all be objectively true. So they *must* be subjective.

Socrates: All of them?

Felicia: Yes.

Socrates: Why couldn't some be true and some false, just as in science? Different physics teachers teach you different things, too, on some issues; not everything is known and agreed on in physics, you know. But that does not prove that physics is merely subjective, does it?

Felicia: No.

Socrates: Then why does it prove that ethics is subjective?

Felicia: But physics is different.

Socrates: How?

Felicia: It's about the real world. Ethics is about our ideals.

Socrates: That is precisely the point at issue. You beg the question again in reducing "the real world" to the physical world and in assuming that ideals are not objectively real, that they are only "ours."

Felicia: But the fact remains that teachers of physics agree a whole lot more than do teachers of ethics.

Socrates: What follows from that, if we grant it to be a fact?

Felicia: That ethics is subjective, of course.

Socrates: Only if you assume another premise again. Do you see which one?

Felicia: Let's see—I'm catching on to this—teachers of ethics disagree, therefore ethics is subjective. That assumes that what teachers disagree about is subjective.

Socrates: Correct. And do you claim that premise is true?

Felicia: Yes. Why not?

Socrates: Because there seem to be many exceptions. In physics, for instance.

Felicia: But physics is different!

Socrates: How?

Felicia: It's about...

Socrates: The real world?

Felicia: Yes. I see. I'm begging the question again. And also my premise is not true. And also I used the term "values" ambiguously. What else can possibly go wrong with my argument?

Socrates: One other thing. Your other premise is also false, it seems: ethical teachers do agree about many things, about basic values. And scientists do not wholly agree.

Felicia: More than ethical teachers, at any rate.

Socrates: Perhaps not even that. Many scientists in the past had very different opinions than most scientists today, didn't they?

Felicia: Yes, but that's disagreement across time. The scientists of any one time largely agree across space.

Socrates: That is true, but what follows from it? Ethical teachers agree across time, and scientists agree across space; do time or space determine truth?

Felicia: I guess not. Well, you've pretty thoroughly demolished my second argument. What about the third one? Aren't you in favor of toleration?

Socrates: I am, but I do not see how the subjectivity of values follows.

Felicia: If you think your values are objective, you'll try to impose them on others.

Socrates: But if they are *not* "my" values, but also real values, then I no more impose them on others than I impose gravity or mathematics on others. They are simply there. Teaching them is like teaching mathematics. As one of your wise men has put it, it's not propaganda but propagation, like old birds teaching young birds to fly.

Felicia: But won't you be much more tolerant if you think values are subjective, and less tolerant if you think they are objective?

Socrates: I think not, and I think I can show you why. Tell me, what modern enterprise do you think has benefited and progressed the most because of toleration and open-mindedness?

Felicia: Science, I suppose.

Socrates: I agree. Now then, does science believe its discoveries are only subjective?

Felicia: No. But it's silly to impose them by force.

Socrates: Yes it is, and it's just as silly to try to impose ethical values by force. The parallel holds.

Felicia: But people tried to do just that in the past; the Inquisition burned heretics.

Socrates: Yes, and other foolish people tried to impose scientific theories by force or threat: the Galileo case, for instance. The parallel still holds. Both fields have their fools.

Felicia: Hmmm. The parallel seems to hold, all right. But maybe the parallel is that they're both subjective. Maybe we were wrong to think science deals with objective truth. Don't today's philosophers of science say that all scientific theories are only conceptual models or myths, relative to the human mind and radically inadequate to reality?

Socrates: Models, yes. Inadequate, yes. Even myths, perhaps. But not subjective, not fantasies. Not humanly invented *worlds*, just humanly invented *words*, or word systems, or pictures. Our way of understanding the physical world is limited and inadequate. So is our way of understanding the spiritual world, the world of values. But both worlds are equally real.

Felicia: Even though our minds are so inadequate?

Socrates: "Inadequate" does not mean "untrue," does it?

Felicia: I suppose not. It seems strange to say ethics deals with *truth* though, as science does.

Socrates: If we believed it didn't, if we thought no ethical teaching could be true, why would we pay attention to it? Values are important to us only if they are true values, isn't that so?

Felicia: I thought values were important to us because of our emotional investment in them. They are our cherished opinions.

Socrates: Opinions about what?

Felicia: What?

Socrates: That is my question, yes.

Felicia: I mean, what do you mean?

Socrates: Is there a reality about which to opine? A referent?

If not, how can there be an opinion? An opinion is an opinion *about* something, and that something is the standard to judge one opinion as closer to it than another. Isn't this how we judge opinions?

Felicia: That would imply an objective truth outside the opinions.

Socrates: Precisely.

Felicia: But we only have opinions, so we don't know the truth.

Socrates: But we want to. The opinion intends the truth, aims at it. It it were not there, how could we aim at it?

Felicia: Oh. Well, then, I guess I don't mean to say that values are *opinions* but *feelings.*

Socrates: The objectivity of values, then, seems to you to be ridiculous because it means the objectivity of feelings, the objectivity of something that is by its essence subjective.

Felicia: Exactly. So you see it as I do after all.

Socrates: Not at all. To me, the *subjectivity* of values is ridiculous because it means the subjectivity of something that is by its essence objective: goods, real goods.

Felicia: How differently we use the same word! Well, then, it's just a matter of preference, of arbitrarily choosing one meaning or another. It's not a thing to argue about. It's subjective. Even your idea of the objectivity of values is just your subjective preference about the word. Neither of us can disprove the other.

Socrates: On the contrary, I think from your own starting point of value-feelings, we can be led to the doctrine of the objectivity of values.

Felicia: How?

Socrates: Consider: what are these value-feelings? Do you not feel called, challenged, "oughted," so to speak, by moral values?

Felicia: You could put it that way.

Socrates: Well, if these values were only subjective, how could they make such demands on you?

Felicia: They come from me. I bind myself by them.

Socrates: If you bind yourself, how are you really bound? You can just as easily loose yourself. Do you feel that you can? Can you be dishonest with a good conscience?
Felicia: No.
Socrates: If you disobey values, they continue to haunt you, to condemn you, to make you feel guilt, don't they?
Felicia: Yes.
Socrates: Now that doesn't feel like the rules of a manmade game, does it? If you change the rules of a game of tag, do you feel guilt?
Felicia: No. But didn't Kant come up with some clever explanation of how we bind ourselves by morality?
Socrates: He distinguished two aspects of the self. His "transcendental ego" posited the values for the "empirical ego" to obey. So it's not really binding yourself. You can't simply bind yourself, or obey yourself, or even have responsibilities to yourself. How can you split yourself in two like that?
Felicia: But we always do say things like that.
Socrates: And what do you think you mean by them?
Felicia: I don't know. What do you think?
Socrates: I think you must mean one of two things. Either you are doing what Kant did, and splitting yourself into two selves . . .
Felicia: That can't be. I'm one self. And it's not *part* of me that insists on values; it's simply *me*.
Socrates: Then it must be the second alternative: you are mistaken about the one to whom you are bound, or responsible.
Felicia: You mean I'm putting myself in the place of God?
Socrates: If the shoe fits . . .
Felicia: Hmmm. I'll have to think more about that. Well, there goes my third argument down the tubes. I guess toleration doesn't prove subjectivity, does it?
Socrates: Oh, it's much worse than that. It proves objectivity.
Felicia: How?

Socrates: Very simply. The real value of toleration presupposes real values. Do you say toleration is really valuable?

Felicia: Suppose I don't? Suppose I just say it is my subjective preference to be tolerant?

Socrates: Then suppose I say it is mine to be intolerant?

Felicia: Well, then we differ, that's all.

Socrates: Exactly: that's all. Then we can no longer argue, or even quarrel. We can only fight. It then becomes a contest of wills or weapons, not words, not minds. And then we really do try to "impose our values," as you put it, on each other. Do you choose to do that?

Felicia: Certainly not. I choose to be tolerant.

Socrates: And do you believe this choice of yours to be tolerant is really better than its opposite?

Felicia: Oops. If I say yes . . .

Socrates: Then there is a real "better."

Felicia: And there can't be a real "better" without a real "good," so then there is a real good, an objective value. So I will have to say no, I do not believe my choice to be tolerant is really better than its opposite, intolerance.

Socrates: Do you honestly believe that?

Felicia: Well . . . no. I can't quite brazen that one out.

Socrates: And here is another argument. If you think that toleration of all values and value systems is good, are you not then "imposing your values," your value system, which includes the value of toleration, on other people or other cultures, not all of whom agree that toleration is a value? Many traditional cultures see toleration as a weakness, as a disvalue. So for you to say that everyone ought to be tolerant is for you to say that your value system, with tolerance, is really better than others, without tolerance. Isn't that "imposing your values" on others?

Felicia: I never thought of that.

Socrates: Do so now, please.

Felicia: I don't think that *is* imposing my values on them.

Socrates: Neither do I.

Felicia: What is it, then?

Socrates: I think it is an insight into a real, objective, universal value: toleration. Some cultures and some individuals simply fail to see it. We make mistakes in values, you know, just as we make mistakes in anything else. Or did you think we were infallible in just this one area?

Felicia: No...

Socrates: Well, if you admit that, you admit objectivity.

Felicia: How?

Socrates: A mistake means a failure to know the truth. Where there is no truth, there is no error.

Felicia: But we should tolerate error, not impose the truth.

Socrates: Indeed. Notice what we tolerate: error, not truth. Evil, not good. Lesser evils, necessary evils. So the very word "toleration" presupposes real good and evil.

Felicia: Oh, Socrates, you have tangled me up in my words again. How typically Socratic!

Socrates: You know better than that by now, Felicia. You know the point of my method is not to win the argument but to win the truth, not to defeat the opponent but to defeat the error.

Felicia: But you use language like a rapier, and your opponent always finds herself full of holes. It's an unfair fight.

Socrates: But as I just said, it's not a fight. Or if it is, we're fighting on the same side. And it's not unfair because we are all equally in the web of words, in language, just as we are all equally within the structures of logic. We live in them as we live in air or light or time. They are the same for all. They are not *mine.*

Felicia: I understand, I think. I just don't like to be made a fool of.

Socrates: The only fool is the one who refuses ever to be a fool.

Felicia: Yes, I've learned that too. But what do you mean by saying that even language is objective? Surely we invent languages.

Socrates: Yes, but not language itself. "In the beginning was the Word." It's a nice parallel to morality, in fact: moralities are invented; morality is discovered. Mores are subjective; morals are objective. Positive law is posited by people; natural law is natural, given.

Felicia: Socrates, I am astonished at your clear distinctions and definitions and arguments. I never thought ethics could be done with such clear and simple logic.

Socrates: That was part of your culture's problem: separating the sciences and the humanities so much that logical thought was separated from values, and values from logical thought.

Felicia: I know that the separation between the sciences and the humanities has harmed both.

Socrates: Worse, it has harmed people, who thought about the most important questions in their lives vaguely, and even often praised this vagueness and demeaned logic as a kind of enemy of values, while they reserved clear and tough-minded thinking for the cave.

Felicia: The cave?

Socrates: Plato's cave. The world of the senses.

Felicia: You mean that's all science is? In the cave?

Socrates: Did you think science dealt with values?

Felicia: You just said you wanted to do values logically.

Socrates: You see? You are assuming an identity between science and logical thought, as if only science can use logic.

Felicia: Oh. But you're insulting science by putting it down in the cave.

Socrates: Not at all. It explores the cave very well. But not the larger world outside. You moderns think very clearly about the structure of the atom, but not about the structure of Adam; about the heart of matter, but not about the heart of the matter, the heart of man. You are more rational about the life of fruit flies than about your own lives.

Felicia: I always thought morality couldn't be logical because it was a matter of subjective motive. And that's my fourth argument. Do you mean to say that motive isn't the most important thing in morality? Or that motive isn't mysterious?

Socrates: No, but I do mean to say that mysteries are to be explored, not ignored.

Felicia: So morality *is* a matter of motive. And motive is subjective. So morality is subjective. See? I can syllogize too.

Socrates: And I can distinguish. Morality *is* motive, but not *only* motive. Even if motive is primary, that does not exclude other, secondary aspects of morality—if indeed they are secondary.

Felicia: I don't know whether we need anything secondary after all. Love alone is enough, isn't it? And love is a motive.

Socrates: But is love *only* a motive? Is it not also a deed? And can you separate its motives from its deeds? Can you hate, or rape, or murder, or steal, or bear false witness out of love?

Felicia: No.

Socrates: Do you see? The commandments which specify good and evil acts are ways of specifying loving and unloving motives *too*. Love does not steal, love does not kill, and so on.

Felicia: Love seems to commit adultery.

Socrates: Not the kind the commandments command. Not faithful love, not unadulterated love.

Felicia: I see. But the motive is the primary thing, at least.

Socrates: Yes. But does the primacy of one thing discount second things? The soul is more important than the body, but isn't the body important too? Humanity is more important than nature, but isn't nature precious? You moderns seem to have this tendency to assume that the greater is somehow in competition with the lesser, and to think of only one thing at a time. You don't think of hierarchy and order and balance. Perhaps the Romantics are to blame, for romanticizing revolutionary extremism and scorning our old Greek wisdom of moderation.

Felicia: Moderation sounds so boring, Socrates.

Socrates: It is just the opposite. Extremism is boring. Did you

ever meet a monomaniac? Moderation is exciting because it is
the principle of life itself. Life is a balancing act between dull
and deathly extremes.

Felicia: What extremes?

Socrates: Physically, things like cold and heat, which threaten
the body. Morally, things like cowardice and foolhardiness,
which threaten the soul.

Felicia: So you think Aristotle was right about the Golden
Mean?

Socrates: Yes, but he carried it to extremes. He was moderate
to excess.

Felicia: I think I know at least one thing that doesn't fit moderation and the Golden Mean: love. How can you have too much
love?

Socrates: If I love a stone as much as a man, isn't that too much?

Felicia: Yes, but how can you love a person too much?

Socrates: If I thought you were God and worshiped you, would
that not be loving a person too much? The great rule is to love
your neighbor *as yourself*, isn't it? Do you worship yourself?

Felicia: No. I don't even worship God. I mean, I don't know
whether there is a God to worship or not. But I guess we'd better
save that for another day. First things first. Let's finish our
tutorial.

Socrates: Second things first, you mean, in this case. Well, as
you will. Let's look at your fourth argument. Could you summarize it briefly?

Felicia: Yes. Situations are relative; morality is determined by
situations; so, morality is relative. How's that for brief?

Socrates: For brief, you get an A. For logic, perhaps a C. For one
thing, it does not prove the thesis you are supposed to be arguing for.

Felicia: Sure it does.

Socrates: I thought you were supposed to be trying to prove
that morality was subjective.

Felicia: Yes.

Socrates: But situations are objectively real, aren't they? So even if morality is determined by situations, it is still objective.

Felicia: But it's relative, at least.

Socrates: If it is wholly determined by situations. Once again, I think we must distinguish conditioning from determining. Do you think morality is wholly determined by situations, or only that situations *help* determine morality?

Felicia: I don't know. I never thought of that.

Socrates: Did you ever study Thomas Aquinas's moral philosophy?

Felicia: Of course not. We read only up-to-date authors here.

Socrates: You mean the ones that will become dated very soon. Yes, I see; that is a good part of your problem.

Felicia: What does Aquinas say about situations?

Socrates: Something moderate and reasonable, I think: that there are three things that make a human act good or evil, not just one: the nature of the act itself, the motive, and the situation or circumstances.

Felicia: What's "the nature of the act itself"?

Socrates: Well, whether it's an act of theft or payment, for instance, or whether it's an act of adultery or married love. The moral law specifies good and evil acts. That's the objective and absolute part of morality. The subjective part is the motive and the relative part is the situation. (But even that is not relative to *us;* it's objective.)

Felicia: So all three have to be right for the act to be right?

Socrates: Right. If I give money to a beggar just to show off, the act in itself is good but my motive is not, so it becomes a morally deficient act. Or if I make love to my wife in the wrong situation, for instance when it is medically dangerous, it becomes a morally deficient act.

Felicia: What a sophisticated position! You say old Aquinas came up with this?

Socrates: He is not so old, after all, compared with me. Actually this position is as old as Augustine. Are you surprised at that?
Felicia: Yes.
Socrates: Perhaps that's because you shared the modern myopia about the history of thought that one of your sages has called "chronological snobbery."
Felicia: Don't you believe in progress?
Socrates: Yes, and also in regress; don't you?
Felicia: Do you think ethics has regressed?
Socrates: In this area, yes.
Felicia: Why?
Socrates: Your three most popular modern ethical philosophies each seem childishly oversimplified. Each isolates and absolutizes one of the three parts of morality.
Felicia: You mean legalism and subjectivism and situationism?
Socrates: Precisely.
Felicia: I don't want to defend childishness. But I think my strongest objection is my next one, because it's so simple. Where is the good or evil in the physical act itself? I just don't understand what that could mean. When I look at a physical act, all I see are facts, not values.
Socrates: So you think the values are in your own feelings instead?
Felicia: Yes. We project our feelings out onto things.
Socrates: Surely you don't mean that literally?
Felicia: Why not?
Socrates: Because then you would be saying that when you see a murder, you feel evil and you project your evil feeling out onto the act.
Felicia: Right.
Socrates: But when you see a murder take place, you don't feel evil. You feel that the murder, or the murderer, is evil.
Felicia: Yes, but the feeling is in me. So I find the evil in me.
Socrates: I think you are confusing adjectives with adverbs.

Felicia: Is this what they do at Oxford? Grammatical petti-foggery?

Socrates: No, necessary distinctions. Let me try to explain. If "in me" is adjectival, it modifies the noun "evil," and then when you say "I find the evil in me," you mean that the evil itself is in you, that you are evil. You just admitted that you didn't feel that you were evil, but that the murder, or the murderer, was evil. So that can't be what you mean. The alternative is that "in me" is adverbial. Then it modifies the verb "find," and when you say, "I find the evil in me," you mean only that the act or process of finding the evil is in you, not the object found. But that's what I say too. The evil is objective, the process of finding it is subjective, just as physical facts are objective, but the process of our sensing them is subjective.

Felicia: But where is the evil in the object, then? I just don't understand. How can a *thing* be evil? You apparently believe in God; didn't God make all things good? Is the maker of all things the maker of ill things?

Socrates: Oh, all *things* are good all right. But *acts* are not *things*. We make acts, God makes things.

Felicia: How can the act be evil, then? It's just a physical event.

Socrates: Is it? You don't think the act of murder is a moral event?

Felicia: No. The moral event is in me. What's out there is just the physical event. "There is nothing good or bad, but thinking makes it so."

Socrates: I don't believe you really believe that. Do you think that if I murdered you and I didn't *think* that was an evil deed, then it wouldn't *be* an evil deed?

Felicia: Not in *your* mind.

Socrates: Would I be right or wrong in thinking that?

Felicia: I think you would be wrong, but *you*'d think you were right.

Socrates: That is not what I asked. I asked which of these two opinions, yours or mine, would be true.

Felicia: Both.

Socrates: But they are contradictories. How can contradictories both be true?

Felicia: Neither, then.

Socrates: But of two contradictories, one must be true and the other false.

Felicia: Socrates, I can't answer your logic. But there's something more than formal logic involved here.

Socrates: I agree. But not less. The law of noncontradiction is never abrogated.

Felicia: I don't know about that.

Socrates: Give me an example—real or imagined—of anything real violating the law of noncontradiction.

Felicia: Paradoxes.

Socrates: They are only *apparent* contradictions. Distinguish two meanings and they are resolved.

Felicia: Mysteries, then.

Socrates: Mysteries meaning the unknown?

Felicia: Yes.

Socrates: How can the unknown be *known* to be contradictory?

Felicia: All right, so I can't escape your logic. But I still don't understand the reality. That's more important.

Socrates: I agree. With all three statements.

Felicia: When I look at the act, I see only physical things, squint as I will.

Socrates: What do you look at the act with?

Felicia: My eyes, of course.

Socrates: Which ones?

Felicia: Both of them, of course.

Socrates: You mean you think you have only two?

Felicia: What do you think I am, a monster?

Socrates: No, a human being, but you apparently think you are only an animal. Do you not know you have an inner eye too?

Felicia: What in the world is that?

Socrates: Perhaps not something "in the world" at all. Or perhaps "in the world but not of the world"...

Felicia: Now you're really mystifying me.

Socrates: Sorry. But you have surely heard of "conscience"?

Felicia: Oh, *that.* But that's just my subjective feeling.

Socrates: You don't see it as a *seeing*?

Felicia: No. I see only feeling in conscience.

Socrates: You *see* this feeling then? With your outer eyes?

Felicia: No...

Socrates: Then you do have an inner eye. You just haven't used it well. And you know what happens to any organ, inner or outer, when it is unused, don't you? It atrophies. You need exercise. You see, this is the reason why you did not believe in objective values: you did not see them.

Felicia: That's right. That's what I've been trying to tell you.

Socrates: And I'm trying to tell you that the reason you didn't see them is because you didn't look at them.

Felicia: That's a departure from your Socratic method: telling me instead of questioning me.

Socrates: That's because as you said, the point you need to see lies beyond the realm of merely formal logic. It's like opening your eyes rather than measuring the light.

Felicia: If you're right, it's very embarrassing—a very simple and a very big mistake, isn't it?

Socrates: I think so. Why do you think so?

Felicia: Because if goodness is objective, if there's a goodness outside us and above us that measures us, a standard, a norm, a real ideal, why then it must be God's goodness. Where else could this objective, absolute, universal goodness be? So then I've got to admit a God too.

Socrates: Do you find it hard to follow the leading of the argument to that point?

Felicia: Yes. In fact, my admitting this much to you is amazing.

In effect, I'm confessing to you that I may have reduced the perfection of the Creator to the feelings of a creature, that I've been trying to take the place of God as the standard of goodness. That's not an easy thing to admit.

Socrates: Perhaps the reason it's so threatening concerns your last reason for the subjectivity of values, the one you ended your paper with.

Felicia: You're right. I found both God and objective goodness threatening to my freedom.

Socrates: Then let us examine this last objection, by all means. Shall we try to formulate it first, as simply as possible?

Felicia: All right. How's this—if values are objective, we are not free. We are free. Therefore values cannot be objective.

Socrates: Fine. Now what do you mean by "free"? Free to do what?

Felicia: To create values.

Socrates: Then I agree with your first premise. If values are objective, we would not be free to create them. But then I disagree with your second premise: we are *not* free in this sense. We cannot create values.

Felicia: What kind of freedom do you think we have, then?

Socrates: The freedom to choose between good and evil.

Felicia: Free will, you mean?

Socrates: Yes. Do you believe we have this freedom or not?

Felicia: I do.

Socrates: But if there is no real, objective good and no real, objective evil, and no real, objective difference between the two, then we do not have the freedom to *choose* between these two gifts that are given, but only the freedom to *imagine* them, to make them up as fantasies, feelings or the rules of our little games.

Felicia: I see. I have to choose between the two kinds of freedom.

Socrates: Yes. Why did you want to create values?

Felicia: I thought it was grander, and greater. But if the values we make aren't real, it's not so grand after all. In fact, it's pretty paltry. Perhaps that's why modern life is so paltry. Say! Maybe that's why I loved Tolkien's *Lord of the Rings* so much: it's got this assumed background of real, strong, objective good and evil. Maybe I missed that in typical modern literature. But if I decide I was wrong and decide to believe in objective values, won't I miss the other thing, the freedom to create my own values?

Socrates: Will you miss hell?

Felicia: Hell?

Socrates: Yes. In hell they create their own values.

Felicia: How do you know that?

Socrates: I will not tell you that now. But I will tell you more about hell. Everyone there wants to be God. That's why they went there in the first place. Did you think God would force anyone to go there if they didn't want to? No, they all chose it freely. They wouldn't have liked heaven. Too objectively real for them. Too threatening to their "freedom."

Felicia: Ooh! My mistake *was* serious.

Socrates: Yes. More than a logical fallacy. That is why I departed from my usual Socratic method to try to free you from it. You see, I put a high value on freedom too.

Felicia: Don't you ever yearn for the other kind of freedom, the freedom to create new values?

Socrates: Instead of answering that question directly, let me do it by asking you one. Do you know any group of people who never yearn for freedom but for bondage instead? Who wants not to be free but to be bound?

Felicia: I don't know. What a silly thing to want! What silly people they must be! Who are they?

Socrates: Lovers.

Felicia: Oh! They *don't* talk about freedom, do they?

Socrates: No. And do you know why?

Felicia: No. Why?

Socrates: Because they are already free.

Felicia: It takes time getting used to this new way of seeing things, you know. A part of me still wants to create my own values.
Socrates: Let's see whether we can use the light of logic again to educate that part of you. Those values you want to create, are they good ones or bad ones? Do you want to create good values?
Felicia: Of course.
Socrates: Then even when you want to create values, you are admitting objective values, a real standard of good and bad to which you want your manmade values to conform.
Felicia: I guess I wasn't the thoroughgoing apostle of subjective values that I thought I was.
Socrates: The thoroughgoing apostate? No.
Felicia: Thank you for helping me to know my true self.
Socrates: That is my mission, to others as to myself.
Felicia: And thank you for going beyond your method of logical questioning for a while and giving me some answers.
Socrates: It hasn't stopped your questioning, has it?
Felicia: No, the answers have created many more questions. That's why I think I'm going to take some religion courses here, just as Peter Pragma decided to do.
Socrates: You realize, of course, that religion is not a *course*?
Felicia: What is it, then?
Socrates: It's a relationship.
Felicia: Something like my relationship with Peter? Oh, did I tell you, we're going out with each other now. We used to be the worst of enemies—he called me a jellyfish and I called him an icicle—and now we're the best of friends. It's like he supplies the bones and I supply the flesh for a single body. I think being in love helped me to understand a lot of those things about God. Well, I've only begun—both relationships—and I've got a long way to go and a lot to learn.
Socrates: You have learned Lesson One very well, Felicia. And at the end of the road you are now beginning lies the realization of your name.

Outline of Arguments in the Dialog on "Objective Values"

Objections:

1. Values are relative to cultures.
2. Society conditions values in us.
3. Moral subjectivism produces toleration.
4. Morality is a matter of subjective motive.
5. Morality is a matter of relative situations.
6. We find no moral values in objects.
7. If we are free, we create values.

Replies:

to 1:   1. Distinguish value-opinions (which are culturally relative) from values (which are not).
   2. Even value-opinions are not wholly relative to cultures; disagreement on applications presupposes agreement on principles.
   3. Moral argumentation presupposes agreement on principles.
   4. The ad hominem argument: even the subjectivist expects objective justice from the objectivist.

to 2:   1. Society conditions opinions but not values.
   2. Not everything we learn from society (teachers) is subjective.
   3. There is a parallel between ethics and physics, even regarding disagreement; disagreement does not prove subjectivity.

to 3:   1. The value of toleration does not logically entail subjectivism.

2. The value of toleration presupposes real values.
3. It is intolerant to refuse to tolerate intolerance.
4. We tolerate only evils, presupposing an objective standard.

to 4: 1. Motives are naturally connected with objective deeds.
2. The primacy of motive does not entail the absence of other moral determinants.

to 5: 1. Situations are objective, not subjective.
2. Situations are only one of three moral determinants.

to 6: We see values by the inner eye of conscience.

to 7: 1. We do *not* have freedom to create values.
2. Free will presupposes an objective good/evil distinction.
3. Freedom to create your own values is hellish, not heavenly.
4. Lovers yearn to be bound, not free; they *are* free.

Postscript

NEWS ITEM: An unprecedented event in American history occurred today at Desperate State University. Representatives of the American Civil Liberties Union and Moral Majority agreed and cooperated on a public issue. Together they obtained a restraining order prohibiting a man identified only as "Socrates" from appearing on the campus of Desperate State. Described by some students as "a teacher without a classroom" and others as "the guru to end all gurus," Socrates had apparently wandered around the campus for the past few weeks "corrupting the minds of the young," according to the Moral Majority people, and proving himself "an enemy of the people," according to the ACLU.

A small group of students staged an orderly protest as Socrates was escorted off campus and taken to the psychiatric ward of General Hospital. Instead of shouting and waving placards, they attempted (in vain) to engage the police, city officials, and ACLU and Moral Majority representatives in debate. The group was led by two of Socrates' followers, Peter Pragma and Felicia Flake, who yesterday had announced their engagement. They vowed to carry on Socrates' work.